T0094337

Coaching Online

Translating traditional coaching methods and competencies for use in the online world, this informative and timely guide shows coaches how to transform their face-to-face practice into one that utilises technological means of communication with clients, mentors, and everyone else associated with their practice.

The book offers up-to-the-minute practical and ethical information from two world-expert coaches, leaning on their combined 50 years of experience and study. It covers the practice of online coaching via email, chat, audio/telephone and video methods, as well as the ethics of online coaching (including an ethical framework), case material, supervision, mentoring and training, and a look into the future of the coaching profession in light of technological developments and the culture of Cyberspace.

Whether you are a coach-in-training or established Coaching Master, this book is an accessible and invaluable tool for taking and maintaining your coaching services online.

Dr Kate Anthony is Fellow of BACP, ISMHO and ACTO, and is CEO of the Online Therapy Institute, which trains and mentors practitioners in the use of technology in mental health and coaching services.

Dr DeeAnna Merz Nagel is a licensed psychotherapist and certified coach. She holds several credentials in the healing arts and offers guidance to professionals through mentorship, supervision and coursework.

Coaching Online

A Practical Guide

Kate Anthony and
DeeAnna Merz Nagel

 Routledge
Taylor & Francis Group

LONDON AND NEW YORK

First published 2022
by Routledge
2 Park Square, Milton Park, Abingdon, Oxon OX14 4RN

and by Routledge
605 Third Avenue, New York, NY 10158

Routledge is an imprint of the Taylor & Francis Group, an informa business

© 2022 Kate Anthony and DeeAnna Merz Nagel

British Library Cataloguing-in-Publication Data
A catalogue record for this book is available from the British Library

Library of Congress Cataloging-in-Publication Data
Names: Anthony, Kate, author. | Nagel, DeeAnna Merz, author.
Title: Coaching online : a practical guide / Kate Anthony and
    DeeAnna Merz Nagel.
Description: Abingdon, Oxon ; New York, NY : Routledge, 2022 |
    Includes bibliographical references and index.
Identifiers: LCCN 2021022366 | ISBN 9781138917453 (hbk) |
    ISBN 9781138917422 (pbk) | ISBN 9781315685939 (ebk)
Subjects: LCSH: Executive coaching. | Technological innovations. |
    Web-based instruction.
Classification: LCC HD30.4 .A626 2022 | DDC 658.4/07124—dc23
LC record available at https://lccn.loc.gov/2021022366

ISBN: 978-1-138-91745-3 (hbk)
ISBN: 978-1-138-91742-2 (pbk)
ISBN: 978-1-315-68593-9 (ebk)

DOI: 10.4324/9781315685939

Typeset in Times New Roman
by Apex CoVantage, LLC

This book could not have been written without the support of our families, colleagues and friends, specifically Dr Stephen Goss of OTI and Jacky Thorne of Wordsmith Services.

DeeAnna is particularly grateful to Ellen Neiley Ritter, Lyn Kelley and Natalie Tucker Miller for inspiration as she entered the coaching profession a decade ago, and for ongoing support throughout the years.

Kate would also like to dedicate this book to Carolina Frohlich, Executive Coach, whose wisdom and coaching skills have been instrumental in her work during the 2020 pandemic and beyond.

As we write, we remember all who lost their lives to COVID-19.

Contents

About the authors

Dr Kate Anthony is a Fellow of BACP, ISMHO and ACTO, and is CEO and co-founder of the Online Therapy Institute. Her doctoral thesis *Developing Counselling and Psychotherapy in the Age of Technology and the Internet* was awarded by Metanoia Institute/Middlesex University in 2010. She is the author or co-editor of five textbooks on the field, as well as publishing many articles and chapters over the last 20+ years. Her core MSc training was with Greenwich University, and she also has a BSc (Hons) in Psychology. Kate's Certified Cyber Therapist course is available at www.kateanthony.net, and is also available as a Young People specialism. The Online Therapy Institute also offers training in Online Supervision, Group Work, Coaching and Virtual Reality. Kate was co-author of all three editions of the *BACP Guidelines for Working Online* (2001; 2005; 2009) including *Online Supervision*; and is currently on the BACP Digital Technologies Expert Reference Group.

Kate, together with her partner Dr Stephen Goss, has upskilled over 15,000 practitioners to work online since lockdown began as a result of COVID-19, offered free of financial obligation to the profession. She lives near Uxbridge in London on a wide beam barge on the Grand Union Canal.

DeeAnna Merz Nagel is the co-founder of the Online Therapy Institute and has partnered with Kate Anthony in co-writing and co-editing books, multiple book chapters, articles, a magazine and curricula for nearly two decades. She has a B.S. in Mental Health & Human Services and M.Ed. in Rehabilitation Counseling. DeeAnna is a Licensed Mental Health Counselor (LMHC) in the state of New York; a Board-Certified Coach (BCC) through the Center for Credentialing and Education (CCE); and an International Association of Coaching (IAC) Masteries Practitioner™. She holds several additional certifications in the healing arts. DeeAnna is a counsellor and coach educator offering courses through the Online Therapy Institute and Institute for Life Coach Training. She has recently completed doctoral studies in Spiritual Direction. Additional information is available at www.deeannamerznagel.com

Including Kate's recent effort during the COVID-19 pandemic in the United Kingdom, Kate and DeeAnna have trained tens of thousands of coaches and therapists across the globe through online courses, live workshops, webinars and keynotes. Their work has been highlighted in the media, including *The Guardian* and the *New York Times*.

Preface

The authors would like to draw attention to the timing of the writing of this book. This took place during the third lockdown in the United Kingdom, while the COVID-19 pandemic continued to wreak havoc globally.

At the time of writing, coaching work taking place face to face has been near impossible for 12 months, only taking place with strict social distancing rules and personal protective equipment, including thorough wipe down of chairs between clients with sanitiser.

Most professionals have made the switch to working online with various degrees of enthusiasm, ranging from outright rejection to positive curiosity about efficacy.

We have sought not to mention the 2020 pandemic too often, as there is currently still hope that it will recede and a return to face-to-face work as standard will be possible. However, it is likely that the pandemic 'hangover' will last for many years and meeting face to face will remain anxiety-provoking and potentially unsafe.

Whether you have decided to move online because of COVID-19, or were already an established online coach looking to update your skills and knowledge base by the purchase of this book, we wish you well with your future career online secure in the knowledge that you know where to turn for the expertise you need. We encourage all coaches to consider blended approaches for communicating with clients in the future.

Kate Anthony and DeeAnna Merz Nagel, Online
Therapy Institute (affiliated with Online Coach Institute).

Acknowledgements

With thanks to Julian Leff (1938–2021), whose work exemplified creativity using technology in the mental health field, and whose kindness in sharing his work will be missed by the authors.

We have colleagues to thank for allowing us to reproduce their work, including Darlene Ouimet, John Wilson and Ellen Neilly Ritter.

Introduction

Nearly a decade ago, the Online Therapy Institute established a *Blueprint for Starting an Online Therapy or Coaching Practice: 25 Questions to Consider* (Nagel and Anthony, 2013). Our goal was to bring focus to the skill and intention needed in becoming an online coach. What follows is a list of these questions, modified for this practical book about online coaching. The contents of this book answer each of these so that a skilled coach can feel confident about delivering services via distance technology:

1 Do you have a basic understanding of the historical timeline regarding the delivery of mental guidance services online?
2 Have you read any of the professional literature and research regarding online coaching?
3 Are you clear about the necessary skillset an online coach should have?
4 Do you have an expectation that your client will have a particular skill online?
5 Do you know what you will do if a client in crisis contacts you?
6 Are you familiar with your responsibilities in maintaining a professional online presence?
7 Do you know what items should be included on an online coach's website?
8 Do you know what additional items you might include in your coaching contract regarding the use of technology and social media?
9 Do you know how you will assess and plan goal setting for an online client?
10 Do you know what method of delivery you will use (email, chat, audio, video, virtual)?
11 Have you had any training with regard to services delivered via technology?
12 Do you believe that online relationships are as real and impactful as in-person relationships?
13 Are you familiar with the Online Disinhibition Effect and how that might impact your work with clients?
14 Do you know how to keep your client motivated between online sessions?
15 Are you clear about your boundaries and availability online?
16 Are you familiar with encryption strategies and solutions online?
17 Have you considered the costs associated with conducting online coaching?

DOI: 10.4324/9781315685939-1

18 Will you charge a different fee for online coaching with proper justification?
19 Will you practice in-person as well as online?
20 Will you require an in-person session prior to seeing someone online?
21 Are you familiar with the nuances of text-only coaching?
22 Have you thought about how your coaching model will fit (or not) with your preferred method of delivery?
23 Do you know about local laws that may impact your online practice?
24 Do you know whether your profession or professional organisation views online coaching as ethical?
25 Are you familiar with 'best practice' standards regarding the provision of coaching?

You can use these questions as a guide while reading the book or, once your reading is complete, revisit them for the purposes of self-evaluation.

Summary of chapters

Chapter 1: cyberculture and its impact on the coaching field

In Chapter 1, we focus on how we and our clients live and work today in cyberspace. We look at how embedded technology is within our lives and hopefully foster a sense of embracement rather than rejection. We recognise the forthcoming tipping point, when coaches in general do not remember times pre-Internet and will probably look back with puzzlement at suspicions of working online. Talk of online therapeutic methods being included in core therapy trainings is already happening in the United Kingdom at the time of writing, with coaching likely to be close behind.

We use the concept of cyberculture to introduce you to thinking ethically as a coach within that culture, using headings to introduce you to those elements of being a modern coach that did not necessarily apply to an off-line world.

Chapter 2: defining coaching and distinguishing it from counselling

In Chapter 2 we look at a brief definition of coaching and how this differs from counselling or psychotherapy. We look at the Masteries of the main international Coaching Professional Bodies in detail, and examine the journeys of the many therapists who have moved into the coaching space. For the therapist wishing to practice both coaching and counselling, we offer advice on who to consult before offering both types of intervention. The blurring of boundaries between the two professions has led us to believe that coaching is, in fact, a subspecialty of counselling.

Chapter 3: working without a physical presence (with text)

Chapter 3 focuses on the technologies used in the early days of the Internet, namely text-based technologies such as email, chat and the many forums and discussion boards that sprung up early on in the Internet's 25+ years of history. Even as a coach using communication methods with a physical or aural presence (telephone, video), it is likely that you will use text to communicate with your client if only from the point of view of logistics. We discuss the ten rules of Netiquette, written to help 'newbies' acclimatise to using such a vast resource alongside others from all over the world.

We also show you the basic techniques of using keyboard text to indicate intended meaning, which is harder without a tone of voice or physical gesture to ameliorate it.

Chapter 4: practical issues in coaching

Chapter 4 returns to the practicalities of text-based coaching via email and chat, before looking at using audio methods such as the telephone and Voice over Internet Protocol (VoIP). We then go on to examine practical tips and tricks for offering a videoconferencing service. We use a case vignette from a colleague to illustrate how she incorporated technology into service delivery and discuss the concept of blending technologies (including face-to-face work) to offer a fully rounded coaching service that aims to meet the client within the practicalities of day-to-day living and working.

Chapter 5: applying the IAC coaching masteries to online coaching

To further illustrate the practicalities outlined in Chapter 4, we offer our own work and how it looks within the IAC Masteries when applied to the online environment. We bring the competencies to life – for example from the client's first search online for a coach and how a website can create that safe space even in these early stages. We look at the coaching contract in depth, offering examples of content you may like to use based on the authors' own practice.

Chapter 6: the ethical framework for the use of technology in coaching

In Chapter 6, we offer you the Online Therapy Institute's own Ethical Framework to refer to during your work and discuss the pros and cons of using social media when one is an online coach. From Directory Listings to the nuances of Twitter, we pose ethical scenarios for you to consider and resolve with our help. We look at other avenues of anxiety-provoking events when one is working online, such as how to respond to the crisis email that arrives in the early hours of the morning.

Chapter 7: essential psychosocial aspects of cyberculture

One of the pleasures of the field, in the authors' experience, is living through the changes and developments in the technologies and seeing the consistencies in human behaviour within those technologies. We have narrowed these down to four essential aspects: Perceived Anonymity, Disinhibition, Telepresence and the natural tendency we have to fill gaps in light of incomplete information (which we call fantasy with a small F). This chapter examines each of these phenomena as it is applicable to your coaching work.

Chapter 8: creating a CPD programme as an online coach

We use Chapter 8 to discuss what Continuing Professional Development (or Continuing Education [CE]) looks like for the online coach. We look at types of formal and informal training programmes and events; peer-reviewed published books and nonacademic resources such as blogging and microblogging. We note the changing face of CPD activities and how self-published materials are now given much more validation than in previous years. We illustrate this point through considering a blog from a colleague which, although written for others, resulted in changing her life.

Chapter 9: a look to the future and concluding thoughts

As the book draws to a close, we turn to the application of technology that seems relevant to the future of the coaching profession in terms of available communication tools. We consider the work of Julian Leff, a psychiatrist whose work exemplifies creativity using technology in the mental health field. We also address the concept of Hologram Coaching in the future, a development that may well bring all practice in-person while still at a distance. We acknowledge such predictions can, however, be rash.

The book ends with an invitation to consider, or reconsider, the questions above. It offers additional questions as points for further consideration as you start, or continue, your journey through cyberspace.

Reference

Nagel, D.M. and Anthony, K. (2013). *A Blueprint for Starting an Online Therapy or Coaching Practice: 25 Questions to Consider*. www.onlinetherapyinstitute.com/startup-blueprint/ [accessed 10 March 2021].

Chapter 1

Cyberculture and its impact on the coaching profession

Introduction

We live in a digital culture, with our coaches swimming in a world of electronic communication and devices unprecedented in the history of human lifestyle and work practice. Where once a handwritten letter, or at a push a telegram, was the normal way to reach each other (and before that carrier pigeon or smoke signals!), we now use electronic mail, an instant messaging programme, a direct message on one of the many social media platforms, or a text message via our mobile phones. We can add our voices to the medium and add video to enhance the process. It has become rare that we are not contactable using some form of technology and it takes a determined person to keep it that way (known as being 'off-grid').

With the rise of technological avenues of communication and ways of seeking information has come a raft of new issues for us as a community in the developed parts of the world. We have new levels of stress in light of information overload, new demands on us being available at any time of day or night and new issues that impact on us emotionally, such as bullying by strangers. In the 25+ years that the World Wide Web has existed, whole generations have grown up not knowing a world where these concerns did not exist. Yet the professions that seek to help a human in life and work have barely noticed the huge shift in how we live and work. This should be a huge concern for those of us in the coaching profession, and also its affiliated professions of counselling, therapy and other mental health areas.

There are many who would argue that the word 'cyberculture' itself is now outdated and irrelevant, but we choose to use it here simply to define that digital world that we now inhabit in the context of coaching and mentoring clients. Put simply by Wikipedia (as of February 2021):

> Internet culture, or cyberculture, is a culture that describes the many manifestations of the use of computer networks for communication, entertainment, and business, and recreation.

We should pause here to note that the author did not reach for a textbook to find that simple definition; she opened a new tab on her preferred browser and typed

DOI: 10.4324/9781315685939-2

the word, before right-clicking and selecting what came up to make it appear in the first draft of this book. This is a good example of how living in a cyberculture works – access to seemingly unlimited resources available at our fingertips, which are accepted as a normal way of gathering information. In addition, this information can be accessed via a multitude of electronic devices – PCs, laptops, tablets, smartphones, and increasingly the appearance of wearable technology such as wristwatches.

Society has tended to fall into one of two camps as the culture of technological use developed: those who resisted it encroaching more and more into how we work and live, and those who embraced it doing so. In our experience, the field of coaching has landed between the two – awareness of it happening and resistance to welcoming it as a tool with which to work with our clients in full. This has been mirrored in the sister fields of counselling and therapy, although we recognise that there will be a tipping point at which there are no coaches or therapists who remember a world pre-Internet. What this chapter endeavours to do is not convert the reader into zealotry regarding using technology, but rather to help recognise that even the hardest resistance to technology cannot be useful to the modern coach if they contract with clients for whom the use of it is a way of life.

How technology has shaped our modern lives

As coaches, we tend to be more aware of the need to maintain a work-life balance and the need to look after ourselves holistically. This will of course look different for different individuals and encompass anything from early morning fresh smoothies and walks on the beach; using essential oils or other life-enhancing techniques or ensuring frequent face-to-face contact with groups of a like-minded social intention. We work hard to ensure our life is in balance, incorporating family life and children, our clients, our homesteads, physical environments and nourishment from academic or professional pursuit. In looking after ourselves and our minds, we can ensure that we are fit to practice with other individuals who are seeking to attain, if not the same way of living, then at least a more positive version of the one they have. Put simply, if there was nothing to improve, they are unlikely to have sought out a Life or Career Coach.

However, our lives have changed immeasurably in light of being permanently connected, or at least having the perception of being permanently connected, and this is a way of life and work that has not arrived fully formed on our doorsteps. Technology has seeped more and more into our daily lives and routines until we are so used to its presence that we are lost when it is suddenly removed from us. It is now a rare human being (in countries that have a developed communication structure) that does not carry a mobile or smartphone with Internet access. For example, mobile phone penetration in Africa is higher than some other parts of the world, which has led to the success of money transfer systems such as MPacer in Kenya – a system that at the time of writing is only just being recognised in the Western world.

As coaches, the majority of us have been trained in a non-connected world. The basis of a coaching relationship has generally been to meet physically with another individual to work together, using techniques and strategies that will help the coachee improve their life in some way – be that emotionally, at work or to gain better financial success. This has followed the same traditional lines as a therapeutic relationship in general over decades – a consulting space designed for two or more people to work together using a physical presence.

Interestingly, we have seen a rise in attention to the telephone coaching and therapy relationship only as a reaction to the development of the online relationship. In the United Kingdom, guidelines from the main professional counselling body regarding telephone work (Payne *et al.*, 2006) were introduced only after the second edition of guidelines for online work were published (Anthony and Jamieson, 2005). It is recognised by the authors that telephone coaching has a long and happy place in the profession, but in the context of cyberculture, the landline telephone – although an example of using technology itself – should be considered as an early form of technological communication, rather than an intrinsic game changer as to the way life is lived digitally today.

Core coaching training has little reference to how we actually live. This is not to say that it ignores day-to-day communication methods, which by their very nature need to be referenced, but rather that the field of coaching has not moved forwards in its practical or theoretical foundations to consider how the use of technology itself has impacted on us, both emotionally and in relation to how we attempt to live healthy individual lives whether at work, home or play. It may be true that the modern coach will email homework exercises to the coachee or provide downloadable .pdf workbooks on a USB drive to complete by hand, but these tools remain stuck in how we worked before we were able to take advantage of technology.

Modern coach training needs to look at how, for example, the use of a coaching app will fit into the individual's life, and what the emotional fall out will be in light of that. Will it be a fun tool that makes mood-tracking easier, or will it be yet another electronic task that has to be completed when your coachee would rather be offline completely? If it is the latter, is that forging resentment to the coaching process and possibly you as coach which will impact on the ability to move forwards in changing a life for the better?

As thought leaders in our field, we have constantly made known that in our opinion the use of technology for technology's sake is to be avoided. It may be convenient that video connections mean we do not need to travel or spend precious resources hiring a consulting room, but if the connection to the Internet is poor, resulting in choppy visuals or broken audio, the coaching process will be seriously damaged. Equally, a smartphone app may have millions of pounds or dollars invested in it, be visually pleasing, and have great emojis to represent our delicate state of mind at any given point, but without a solid connection to Wi-Fi it is pretty much rendered useless.

The importance of the empathetic coach

The coach who rejects the use of technology in their life and work is, of course, just as useful as one who embraces it! We do not pretend that such ways of working no longer exist, or that they should be rendered so out-of-date as to be useless – there is a fine tradition of coaching thought and theory that evidences the life-changing power of the coaching process for the individual before the World Wide Web was invented, and as such it still needs to be recognised as the traditional core of what we do. Using technological means within our work should be seen as an improvement rather than a replacement if they are to be used at all.

The coach who chooses not to develop an awareness of the rise of technology needs to carefully consider their relevance to today's profession, and their fitness to practice if they are to work with individuals who do embrace technological tools and increasingly rely on it as a normal facet of life and work. There are many avenues of coaching practice that need no modern devices to improve on the core intentions of the work – the Breathing Coach for example may rely entirely on sitting with a coachee and breathing with them as they teach their techniques! However, if this coachee wishes to use an app to help them maintain their work outside of the session, the coach needs an awareness of how such tools work and what the benefits (and indeed pitfalls) may be as it impacts on the work. At the extreme end, the Breathing Coach who rejects such apps denies the client autonomy in how they wish to work on improving their life and health.

This simple example underlines how we as coaches need to fully appreciate the changes in society as they apply to our work in light of technological advancement, and the advent of the Internet in changing how we communicate on a daily basis. We can reject the use of technology and this need not be a bad way of living; but we will only be able to work with an increasingly small niche of clients with a like-minded way of life. If we cannot empathise with our client, we are rendered unable to appreciate changes in lifestyle and work practices that are probably essential in improving their lives.

These coaches may see many positives in a strategy of telling the client to turn off their phones or their laptops, and to find environments where there are no Wi-Fi hotspots – and as a general strategy in reducing stress levels and combating the overwhelm many of us experience in light of information overload that the Internet affords us, this is often good advice! But to assume that being disconnected permanently is the answer to balancing our lives may be compared to amputating an arm to treat a sprained wrist. For the modern coach, to be effective in helping the client improve their lives is to be able to empathise with that way of life, whether it matches our own preferred way of living or not.

The coach as passionate advocate

Equally, we should not assume that our own passion for connected living and electronic tools is shared by our client. The coach who uses the methods of communication and stand-alone programmes that are available to us in modern society

may find them intensely useful in both their own life and work, and be enthusi-
astic in sharing this with colleagues and family as a benefit as to how they can
enhance our emotional and practical strategies for maintaining a positive way of
being. But the coach as technology zealot when it comes to working with a particular client is rarely a good intervention. There is strong caution to be exercised
when advising a client to (for example) email an employer with a list of changes
they wish to be made in the workplace to improve their own daily practice. There
are well-documented examples of how misinterpretation of the written word can
result in disastrous interpersonal relationships, completely negating the intention
of the coachee in the first place.

There is, however, a good argument for the Internet-savvy coach to be prepared
to educate their clients as to what online or electronically based services there are
when they see a good fit. For example, a client who uses a smartphone may be
unaware of the myriad of different mood-tracking apps that exist and may find
the concept of using the mobile phone as a personal tool attractive. Similarly, the
coach well versed in the many types of online support forums is well placed to give
appropriate links to their client, particularly when the client needs more therapy-
based input in their lives to run alongside the coaching process.

The disinhibited coach

It is also not too early in this book to mention the importance of recognising how
communication over electronic means – particularly considering the fast-paced
nature of such communications – are strongly influenced by what John Suler
named The Online Disinhibition Effect in 2001 (revised in 2004). In our work
in the field of technological use within coaching and other forms of therapeutic
practice, we have come to recognise disinhibition online as being central to the
work in a hugely positive, and equally a hugely negative, way. We shall explore
this theme comprehensively in Chapter 7, but in summary we may view it thus:

The nature of working without a physical presence, or with a physical presence
but at a distance, means that elements of inhibition that shape our daily interactions as being acceptable in society are either diminished or not apparent at all.
Within a coaching or therapy relationship, this is often seen as a positive effect
as the client feels freer to discuss elements of their life and emotions that may
impact on the work. Conversely, it may be seen as a negative effect as they may
display behaviour that is not wise and which they would not display in a face-to-
face situation.

Understanding disinhibition and the impact it has on us as coaches is important.
One of the first written assignments our students have when training is to examine
a situation where they now recognise that they or another were disinhibited – from an
inappropriate Twitter interaction to over-sharing personal information on a professional forum. These occasions become doubly important if they happen using
social media platforms where privacy policies are at best a fluid thing. Human
nature is to be curious, and most clients cannot resist Googling a coach's name

to find out more about them. If this happens, discovering a drunken picture on Facebook or an emotionally charged angry tweet can affect the coaching relationship negatively.

Christofferson (2007) offers a different word for us to better understand the disinhibition effect – catharsis. This more familiar word can help us recognise where clients are finding disinhibition to be non-toxic. She points out that the sense of anonymity that comes with the ability to be disinhibited allows for client autonomy within the session. This also offers the clients space to explore elements of their psyche that would receive social disapprobation off-line. Reading Christofferson's full paper is encouraged.

The well-networked coach

Chapter 6 will look at the use of social media and other online methods as a way to network within a coaching business plan, and here we examine the reasons for doing so. It should be stated that traditional ways of networking remain essential to the rounded coach's well-being. Attending conferences, being part of local networking groups and growing contacts through other professionals are core not only to keeping up to date with movements in the coaching field but also to having a work-based circle of like-minded professionals to discuss ideas, socialise with and share resources. If anything, the advent of the World Wide Web has made this easier. We can join professional networking platforms such as LinkedIn to keep aware of not only coaching-related resources but also new job and career opportunities and training courses to further our CPD. Joining an online coaching group on LinkedIn is the simplest way of being connected, as the site operates on the principle of six degrees of separation (everyone and everything is six or fewer steps away, by way of introduction, from any other person in the world).

The online coach does well to take full advantage of such networking sites. Facebook, although designed originally for social networking, is increasingly used for business purposes – many practitioners and organisations have a Facebook page where online articles of interest and other resources can be shared, as well as reaching out to contacts by their simple use of the ubiquitous 'like' button. Growing an army of followers on Twitter can aid business practice to get both online and offline services noticed, as well as keeping the coach connected to others who share online resources, post motivational quotes, and reach out to other Twitter users.

As well as the well-known networking platforms there are likely to be many other online forums where coaches can take up their online space to keep connected to what is happening in the field and who is also residing there. Attending online conferences, where one can (usually) see and hear the expert presenter while taking part in a chat room conversation about the topic is both a cost-effective method of gaining CPD hours and also a good way of meeting fellow coaches (Wilson and Anthony, 2015). Organising online events is also a good way of growing contacts via an email list, which can then be used not only for networking but also for marketing purposes.

The coach as expert author

Again, Chapter 4 will cover the practicalities of how your online practice can grow using the tools and methods that the Internet has given us, but here we will look at the attitude shift that has occurred when it comes to traditional methods of writing. The two most obvious changes in the publishing world have come in the form of self-publishing eBooks and blogging. These two ways of getting one's writing in front of an audience has exploded the concept of knowing or having an opinion about a topic and publishing it in written form. According to Wikipedia (accessed March 2015), on February 20, 2014, there were around 172 million Tumblr and 75.8 million WordPress blogs in existence worldwide, and those are only two of the popular blog platforms in existence. Essentially, with the advent of the World Wide Web, everyone became a potential expert author.

A blog (a truncation of web-log) is essentially an online journal and works best when constantly added to. They can be subscribed to, have comments added by the general public and in the form of a 'vlog' contain video entries. The entries to a blog essentially revolve around one topic or field, which can be anything from what you have for breakfast to your thoughts around coaching techniques and theories. The popularity of the blog depends on the quality of the writing, whether you have an audience interested in the topic, and can develop a great ongoing dialogue via the comments section. Your thoughts and opinions are as important as they ever were – but now you can have a potentially global audience with which to share them!

E-books have also become increasingly popular (you may well be reading this on a Kindle or other make of e-reader now). Self-publishing no longer has the connotations of 'vanity project' that it once had, and many self-publishers are now famous and rich as a result of their writing (many with movie deals in the world of fiction writing). The Internet-savvy coach not only has an openness to this way of getting their work published but also positively seeks it to reach audiences. Self-publishing takes as much effort as writing a traditionally paper-bound book, but the results are much quicker to produce and the low-cost of doing so can be reflected in the cover price, making your work more accessible than to just those who can afford a textbook.

The coach as virtual tutor

Alongside the many ways of delivering resources and information noted above is how coaching courses themselves can be delivered. While most people would argue that core coaching training can and should only be delivered with the face-to-face coaching practice in mind, and that this should be reflected in the training method, the availability of CPD online should not be ignored. These trainings can take place in a structured way, either synchronously (requiring those involved to be online at the same time) or asynchronously (delivered or accessed at a time determined by the trainee).

Synchronous training courses are usually a mix of course materials made available offline (hand-outs delivered by email, for example), and live webinars or teleconferences (audio and/or video). Each training session has a set topic to be taught, and time can be set aside at the end for co-learning by trainees via discussion in chat rooms or other synchronous communication channels. Scheduling of training sessions generally reflects face-to-face training schedules, that is, weekly meetings. One of the huge benefits of these online trainings is not only that they cut travel and sometimes hotel accommodation costs, but can also reach participants from all over the world, convenience of the geographical time zone permitting.

Asynchronous training courses mean that the matter of time zone convenience can be set aside completely. This makes the course entirely self-paced, designed to fit around the trainee's many other commitments to both work and life outside it. Learning platforms can incorporate all the bells and whistles of audio, video and article downloads, and can easily link to external environments such as virtual reality platforms to incorporate live sessions as bonus material or for networking and co-learning discussions. Written assignments can be completed both within the learning platform and as uploaded documents, which in turn can be accessed by the tutor asynchronously at a time that suits them to give feedback and mentoring. Recorded webcasts or podcasts (audio recordings) fit online trainings well and can break up previously staid text-based formats.

The fully virtual coach

One of the more (currently) unusual ways of working online is to create an avatar – a computer-generated representation of the self – and to inhabit a virtual environment. Probably the best known and most widely used virtual world is Second Life, which can be simply explained as being in a computer or video game without the gaming element. Originally invented as a social platform, Second Life is increasingly used by global organisations and institutions as a second environment to grow company profiles and conduct training in-house for employees, or just to create a social space for internationally disparate members to meet up. Communication is held via text (chat) or voice, with the usual asynchronous message boards and mailing systems in place. Confidentiality for clients' needs to be considered, as the platform was not designed for private interactions, but other virtual reality platforms and worlds exist that have been designed specifically with the coaching, mentoring or therapy practice in mind and therefore have fully encrypted communication channels.

Virtual environments offer a playground for the creative coach to design tools with which their clients can work. Instead of being held to the reality of the physical body, clients can design and create their fantasy persona – one they can aspire to be in the area within which they seek to make improvements or changes. This can be particularly suitable for coaching practices that aim to help with physical changes, such as with weight-loss clients. More traditional elements of coaching practice can be updated to be recognisable in a virtual world – the use of vision or collage boards is particularly successful, as images are not only easily created but they can also be represented by a 3D image to be walked around and explored interactively. Working in this way needs management, and an awareness of some of the more extreme effects such an environment can have on someone who may have elements of instability in their mental health; but for the majority of coaching clients, it can be a vibrant and exciting way of working.

Thinking ethically as a coach within cyberculture

The headings in this chapter are designed to give you an introduction to some of the elements of being a modern coach that we simply did not have to consider before the invention of the Internet and subsequently the World Wide Web. What is important to recognise is that the use of technology in our lives and work is highly unlikely to disappear, and as such we need to embrace it, at least to some extent, for us to be able to function as coaches in modern society. It is worth repeating that this book is not designed to convert you, or even to convince you that technology *must* be used in your work. What we are stressing is that the way our clients perform and grow as human beings is likely to include large elements of technologically mediated communication, and as such we at least need to recognise the function of technology as it affects their work and life performance – both practically and emotionally.

Whatever realm of coaching practice you inhabit, you are likely to have already found the need to adopt a stance and develop a course of action in relation to technological use brought about by living in a digital culture. Your life and work are likely to include the daily use of email, instant messaging and/or texting via a mobile phone, picking up a telephone and setting meetings to be held over a video connection. You may be an avid user of Facebook or be well versed in creating contacts and distributing resources via Twitter. Perhaps you use an online calendar system to organise your week, or a remotely held note-taking and contact list for client appointments. You could have abandoned the concept of needing an office, desk or device wired to the wall completely, managing work and life through a tablet or smartphone. With the technological advancement we have seen in the last 25 years, our ways of working and living have altered radically, and are likely to continue to do so.

As coaches, we have an ethical and moral duty to our clients in all that we do. Our professional organisational affiliations provide us with a concrete approach as to how to behave in an ethical manner within our work, whether the content is referred to as a framework, as masteries or as suggested principles (as just a small example of turns of phrase!). An ethical stance does not change in light of cyberculture and technological use, but it does afford us the opportunity to consider nuances within our client work that we did not face when holding our more traditional face-to-face meetings with clients. These need not be entirely practical nuances, such as whether to use encrypted services when emailing a client; they can also be around looking after your clients' emotional welfare by understanding that disinhibition may be affecting the core work, or that conducting a professional relationship online may foster an intimacy that needs boundaries if it is not to bleed into our personal lives. We cannot escape that we live in a connected society, and to continue to be an effective and ethical coach, we need to find our place within that society, as it relates to our client work in particular.

The practical nuances of offering and conducting a coaching practice using technological tools within ethical boundaries will be addressed fully in Chapter 6, where we offer a revised *Ethical Framework for the Use of Technology in Coaching*, co-authored with Ellen Neilly-Ritter of the Institute for Life Coach Training (ILCT). However, what is intrinsic to offering an online or otherwise technologically mediated coaching service is an understanding of how important it is to have an ongoing awareness of how the technology impacts on both us and our clients, within a mindful framing of what it is we do. We can be Life Coaches, Executive Coaches, Breathing Coaches or otherwise – it is our ability to use our moral judgement and our ability to think critically when using electronically facilitated tools that will protect us from undesired consequences that may come about because of their use.

References

Anthony, K. and Jamieson, A. (2005). *Guidelines for Online Counselling and Psychotherapy*. 2nd Edition, including *Guidelines for Online Supervision*. Rugby: BACP Publishing.

Christofferson, K. (2007). 'The Positive and Negative Implications of Anonymity in Internet Social Interactions: "On the Internet, Nobody Knows You're a Dog"', *Computers in Human Behavior*, 23, pp. 3038–3056.

Payne, L., Casemore, R., Neat, P. and Chambers, M. (2006). *Guidelines for Telephone Counselling and Psychotherapy*. Rugby: BACP Publications.

Suler, J. (2004). 'The Online Disinhibition Effect', *Cyberpsychology & Behavior: The Impact of the Internet, Multimedia and Virtual Reality on Behavior and Society*, 7(3), pp. 321–326.

Wilson, J. and Anthony, K. (2015). 'Immersion Disinhibition: How the Internet Has Changed Our Learning', *Therapeutic Innovations in Light of Technology*, Winter, 2015, pp. 13–18.

Chapter 2

Defining coaching and distinguishing it from counselling

What is coaching? Coaching is a transformative process for personal and professional awareness, discovery and growth (International Association of Coaching [IAC], 2017).

We will start with a brief definition of coaching and how coaching differs from counselling or therapy, before continuing to examine the role of the therapist who has become or is becoming a coach. Wikipedia defines coaching thus (as of February 2021):

> Coaching is a form of development in which an experienced person, called a coach, supports a learner or client in achieving a specific personal or professional goal by providing training and guidance. The learner is sometimes called a coachee. Occasionally, coaching may mean an informal relationship between two people, of whom one has more experience and expertise than the other and offers advice and guidance as the latter learns; but coaching differs from mentoring by focusing on specific tasks or objectives, as opposed to more general goals or overall development.

We prefer to distinguish coaching as different from other helping professions in that coaching focuses on the individual's strengths rather than attempting to correct deficits. Coaching does not involve diagnosis; therefore, coaching stays 'above the wellness line'. Coaching encourages the client to find the answers from within. The coach is often the guide that points the client to what he/she already knows to be relevant and true.

Further definition can be ascertained by understanding coach competencies. Said differently, the competencies represent a knowledge base that is brought to the forefront when assisting a client. For the purposes of this chapter, we shall review the three main international coaching bodies offering accreditation and/ or credentialing:

1   International Coach Federation (ICF)
2   International Association of Coaching (IAC)
3   Center for Credentialing and Education (CCE)

DOI: 10.4324/9781315685939-3

Each of these organisations All three offer guidelines and options for professional development. Detailed information can be found at their respective websites: the ICF's is *coachfederation.org*; IAC's is *certifiedcoach.org* and CCE's *cce-global.org*.

To begin, we will discuss the ICF and the IAC. The same individual, Thomas J. Leonard, the 'Father of Professional Coaching', founded both the IAC and ICF. Leonard founded the ICF in 1995 and the IAC later in 2003.

ICF credentialing emphasises coach training, mentoring and experience, as well as an online test and demonstration of coaching skill. With IAC, the process of certification is streamlined, emphasising the results of coach training, mentoring and experience, rather than the documentation of it. This makes the IAC certification process simpler, but that does not imply that the process is easier as coaches must demonstrate masterful coaching skills. Only some 25% of coaches who apply for IAC Coach Certification pass on the first try. The 'test' for the IAC requires recorded coach sessions to be submitted for review. Upon review, the sessions are critiqued using the IAC's competencies, referred to by the IAC as Masteries™.

The ICF has three levels of coaching credentials: The Associate Credentialed Coach (ACC); the Professional Credentialed Coach (PCC) and the Master Credentialed Coach (MCC). The ICF has two pathways for credentialing: The portfolio route allows you to get your coach training anywhere; and the accreditation path requires you to study at an ICF accredited coach training school. The IAC does not require demonstration of coach training, just the results of it: masterful coaching skills. Most IAC Certified Coaches have had substantial coach training and/or mentor coaching even though such training is not required to apply for the IAC credential.

The third organisation, CCE, is primarily focused on credentialing coaches in the United States although coaches from across the globe may apply for their coaching credential, the Board-Certified Coach (BCC). Created in 1995 as an affiliate of the National Board for Certified Counselors (NBCC), CCE credentials nearly 25,000 practitioners globally in a variety of fields.

The BCC was created in 2010. Qualification towards the BCC is tiered, based on years of experience and educational background. The BCC has been aimed primarily at licensed mental health professionals in the United States. Those licensed mental health professionals who meet their state's licensing standards, who hold a master's degree and hold the required years of supervision, may apply for the BCC having acquired 30 additional hours of coach training. Depending on their educational and experiential background, other candidates can expect to complete 60 to 120 additional hours of training. As with the ICF, training can be obtained from approved providers vetted by CCE. Once the training is complete, the candidate must pass a competency exam.

All three coach organisations described earlier require CE/CPD to maintain the credential.

Coaching as a profession

Coach organisations such as the ICF and IAC have strived to present coaching as a distinct profession that stands apart from their kin in the helping professions (counselling, consulting and mentoring for example). While coaching has roots in psychology, and particularly the field of positive psychology, coach theory and application remains an approach that can stand alone and apart from counselling, consulting and mentoring. As a working example, for comparison we shall examine the distinctions between coaching and counselling. A coach does not refer to disease, diagnosis, pathology or words used within the allopathic medical model. Words and conversation of optimal 'wellness' – spiritual, mental, emotional and/ or physical wellness – are spoken. For counsellors who also offer coaching:

> Will I be able to coach this client without resorting back to my counsellor language? Can I stay above the wellness line?
>
> (Nagel, 2016)

Briefly, the difference is this: counsellors generally work with people who are in a state of dysfunction, and the goal of counselling or therapy is to bring them to a state of function. Coaches do not work with clients who are in a state of dysfunction but rather they work with functioning clients who need guidance with reaching specific life or well-being goals (Patterson, 2008).

Coach training generally focuses on two main tracks: Life, or Health/Wellness Coaching. We will primarily focus on the scope practice of the Life Coach, but it should be mentioned that many other coach approaches exist which include but are not limited to recovery coaching, trauma-informed coaching, cognitive behavioural coaching, intuitive coaching and executive coaching. In fact, as coaching is not regulated, one can determine a niche and brand accordingly (more on regulation in Chapter 4 and niche/branding in Chapter 5).

Competencies expected to be achieved through coach training and experience are delineated within each of these three organisations. For the purpose of this book, we will focus on the competencies set forth by the IAC. The IAC refers to these competencies as The IAC Coaching Masteries™ (please note, in Chapter 6 we will apply these Masteries™ to working online).

This IAC Masteries™ overview and the IAC The Coaching Masteries™ are offered verbatim from their website and PDF download; this information is made freely to the public (International Association of Coaching, 2020).

The purpose of the IAC Coaching Masteries™ is to provide the basis and standards for an independent certifying body, without allegiance to any coach training schools or organisations. Our goal is to create a vehicle for evaluating effective coaching in the moment. Specifically, the IAC certification focuses on masterful coaching skills that are observable and can be measured by our certifiers during recorded, half-hour sessions with two different clients.

The IAC Coaching Masteries™ was developed by an international team of coaches with the aim of producing clear standards and measures for what constitutes the highest level of coaching, and that can be understood in any culture around the world.

IAC The Coaching Masteries™

1 Establishing and maintaining a relationship of trust

Definition

Ensure a safe space and supportive relationship for personal growth, discovery and transformation.

Effect

1   The client is open to sharing and receiving.
2   The client perceives the coach as a personal advocate.
3   The client sees transformation and growth as manageable.
4   The client has realistic expectations of results and responsibilities of coaching.

Key elements

1   Mutual respect and acceptance.
2   Confidence and reassurance.
3   The client feels safe to share fears without judgement from the coach.

2 Perceiving, affirming and expanding the client's potential

Definition

Recognises and helps the client acknowledge and appreciate his or her strengths and potential.

Effect

1   The client has greater appreciation of personal capabilities and potential.
2   The client is more willing to take actions beyond current paradigms or strategies.

Key elements

1   Being in empathy with the client.
2   Recognising a wider range of possibilities.
3   Encouraging and empowering the client.
4   Challenging limiting beliefs.

5 Recognising strengths of client and awareness of where strengths support personal and organisational goals (where appropriate)

3 Engaged listening

Definition

Give full attention to the words, nuances and the unspoken meaning of the client's communication; the coach is more deeply aware of the client, his/her concerns and the source of the issue, by listening beyond what the client can articulate.

Effect

1 The client feels understood and validated – not judged.
2 The client communicates more effortlessly and resourcefully.

Key elements

1 The coach focuses on what the client expresses, both verbally and nonverbally.
2 The coach listens beyond what the client articulates.
3 The coach is alert to discrepancies between what the client is saying (words) and the client's behaviour and/or emotions.

4 Processing in the present

Definition

Focus full attention on the client, processing information at the level of the mind, body, heart and/or spirit, as appropriate. The coach expands the client's awareness of how to experience thoughts and issues on these various levels, as and when appropriate. The coach utilises what is happening in the session itself (client's behaviour, patterns, emotions, and the relationship between coach and client etc.) to assist the client towards greater self-awareness and positive, appropriate action.

Effect

1 The client is free to express and engage with present reality.
2 The client is unencumbered by past or future preoccupations or concerns.
3 The client benefits from coaching insight and support on all levels.
4 The coach is highly attuned to subtle communications from the client.

Key elements

1 The coach is aware of the dynamics occurring within the session, within the client and between coach and client and understands how the dynamics are affecting the client and the coaching.

2   The coach has a simultaneous and holistic awareness of the client's communications at all levels.
3   The coach can discern whether the client is communicating from the past, present, or future.
4   The coach allows the client the opportunity to process and clarify the coach's questions and comments.
5   The coach allows the client the opportunity to process his or her own thoughts and responses.

5 Expressing

Definition

Attention and awareness to how the coach communicates commitment, direction, intent and ideas – and the effectiveness of this communication.

Effect

1   The coaching interaction is enhanced with the client being at ease and trusting.
2   The client is open to understand and/or question any communication from the coach.

Key elements

1   Respect
2   Attentiveness
3   Client-focused
4   Clarity
5   Appropriateness

6 Clarifying

Definition

Reduce/eliminate confusion or uncertainty; increase understanding and the confidence of the client.

Effect

1   The client and the coach move forwards in a more directed way.
2   Increased possibilities.
3   Decreased uncertainty.
4   Uncovering the unknown.

Key elements

1 Identify the most important issues while respecting client's preferences and limitations.
2 No judgement by the coach, no leading towards a particular destination.
3 Identify key values and needs.
4 Facilitate alignment of purpose, vision and mission.
5 Identify blocks to progress.

Helping the client set and keep clear intentions

Definition

Helps the client become or remain focused and working towards intended goals.

Effect

1 The client feels capable.
2 The client is clear about what he or she wants to accomplish or transform.
3 The client is inspired by the possibilities.
4 The client moves forwards purposefully.

Key elements

1 Enquiring into the client's intentions and goals.
2 Staying mindful to what is most important.
3 Clarifying direction of progress.
4 Periodically reviewing, revising and/or celebrating the process and intentions.

7 Inviting possibility

Definition

Creating an environment that allows ideas, options and opportunities to emerge.

Effect

1 The coach enables expansion of thoughts and actions.
2 The client's awareness is expanded.
3 The coach helps client transcend barriers.
4 The client is willing to leave his/her comfort zone.
5 The client has more options.

Key elements

1 Trust, openness, curiosity, courage and recognition of potential.
2 The coach and the client communicate through exploration and discovery.
3 Identify 'internal' possibilities (e.g. personal greatness, higher purpose) and 'external' possibilities (e.g. resources, memes).
4 Possibilities are generated by the coach, the client, or a collaboration of the two.

8 Helping the client create and use supportive systems and structures

Definition

Helping the client identify and build the relationships, tools, systems and structures he or she needs to advance and sustain progress.

Effect

The client is confident and secure in moving forwards, knowing that resources are available or can be created.

Key elements

1 The coach suggests possible support systems and structures appropriate to the client's needs.
2 The coach prompts the client to identify support systems and structures the client has but is not utilising effectively.
3 The coach assists the client to identify areas in which the client feels a need for support and structure.
4 The client understands the value of appropriate support systems.

5 The client's progress towards their goals or intentions is more sustainable.

For current competencies/standards set out by the ICF and CCE, please visit their respective websites.

Therapist as a coach

It would be remiss not to acknowledge that the field of professional coaching is filled with therapists who have moved into the coaching space. The following is summarised from an article written by the authors, with updated key points and suggestions (Anthony and Nagel, 2011).

Legally, it depends on *who* is defining counselling and coaching. Theoretically, there are differences (Nagel, 2016) and from a risk management perspective for licensed or registered practitioners, the concern is that the practitioner truly knows how to extract purest coaching from the broadest definition of counselling:

> Counselling and psychotherapy are mainly, though not exclusively, listening-and-talking-based methods of addressing psychological and sometimes psychosomatic problems, including deep and prolonged human suffering, situational dilemmas, crises and developmental needs, and aspirations towards the realisation of human potential . . . and may be concerned not only with mental health but with spiritual, philosophical, social, and other aspects of living.
>
> (Feltham and Hanley, 2017).

It is this broader definition that someone would be called to answer to should a complaint go before a licensing board, a sanctioning board or, in the case of a lawsuit, a judge. Additionally, what has developed is two different opinions – the first is that coaching and counselling are two separate and distinct disciplines. The other opinion that has emerged both in the United States and in the United Kingdom is the idea that coaching is in fact a sub-specialty of counselling.

The CCE is an affiliate of the National Board of Certified Counselors (NBCCs) and has offered the Board-Certified Coach Credential since 2011. With the development of the Coaching Division of the BACP in 2010, the fields of counselling and coaching seem to have further blurred the areas of separate and distinct fields of practice. Professionals in both the coaching and counselling disciplines sometimes struggle with this blurring, and the lines of demarcation are becoming less and less obvious. Therapists who are licensed or registered might choose to use coaching techniques and tools, or even gain a coaching credential, but still identify as a counsellor. The concern is that there is a misconception that a licensed mental health practitioner can simply call themselves a coach by gaining a coach credential and practising coaching across state or international borders.

As a licensed or registered practitioner, this would be risky because of the broad definition of counselling referred to above. A counsellor should accept the idea that one should be professionally trained as a coach because to do otherwise suggests working outside of one's scope of practice; the counsellor believes that the rules of the mental health license or professional organisation are the guidepost. However, these issues may be more legal than ethical in nature. Ethically, we can certainly separate coaching and counselling into two professions and create different contracts and recommend different websites for coaching and counselling services. But when we think in terms of verbatim material, it becomes clear that a therapist who is also a coach must keep the purest methods of coaching in mind so that the verbatim transcript is evidence of coaching and not counselling. It does not matter how different the language is during a coaching session – if it is positive psychology, it is still embedded in psychological interventions. If it is motivational in nature, it is still rooted in psychological interventions. If the goal is to help, aid and guide someone to a different outcome, then by the very general definition previously offered, and by even more stringent definitions of counselling, it will be regarded as counselling in the event ANY complaint is filed and goes forwards.

Coaches must understand that if they are also licensed or registered as a mental health practitioner, should a complaint or lawsuit ensue the practitioner will be held to the highest standard of care.

Should a therapist wish to practice both coaching and counselling, the following is advised:

1 Consult with your regulatory board.
2 Consult with your professional association.
3 Consult with your malpractice insurance.
4 Consult with your lawyer.

If you are advised that you can proceed, document your consultations as proof of due diligence in determining your professional responsibilities. These consultations indicate good practice management and allow you to assess your risk. Some may see this as an issue only in the United States – the battle of the regulated versus non-regulated helping professions – and yet the more global picture is perhaps indicative of a merge between the two disciplines. Lack of regulation of both therapists and coaches in the United Kingdom may make it seem that this topic is less relevant to those practicing outside the United States, but it is important to consider that complaint procedures are extremely relevant. The emergence of the BACP Coaching Division brought to light much speculation on social networking sites at the time as to whether the main professional organisation's name might change to the British Association for Counselling, Coaching and Psychotherapy (or similar), and whether there would be a new membership grade for coaches. Statements from BACP during these discussions indicated that this was not on the cards, and since that time, this has not come to pass.

References

Anthony, K. and Nagel, D. (2011). 'Coaching & Counselling – Is There a Merge of Disciplines on the Horizon?', *Therapeutic Innovations in Light of Technology*, 2(1), pp. 24–29.

Feltham, C. and Hanley, T. (2017). *The SAGE Handbook of Counselling and Psychotherapy*. London: Sage.

IAC Masteries™ (2007–2017). https://certifiedcoach.org/certification-and-development/the-coachingmasteries/ [accessed 8 February 2021].

Nagel, D.M. (2016). 'In the News: What Is the Difference between a Coach and a Therapist?', *Employee Assistance Report*, 19(8), p. 7.

Patterson, J. (2008). *Counselling vs. Life Coaching* (online). https://ct.counselling.org/2008/12/counselling-vs-life-coaching-2/ [accessed 8 February 2020].

Chapter 3

Working without a physical presence (with text)

Authors' note: Adapted and updated from Anthony and Nagel (2010)

Introduction

If you already practice online as a coach, it is likely you use more sophisticated tools than just text, such as telephone and/or video. However, such technologies are relatively recent on the historical timeline of online coaching and their popularity masks what we have learnt from the early days of the Internet when the only communication technology available to us was text: via email, chat rooms, online forums and discussion boards.

As these early days of using Internet communication with clients concentrated on the use of text, the most frequent question coaching practitioners have had is *how* it was possible to work without a physical presence, including an aural one. In this chapter, we will see how this is possible, drawing on the concepts from Chapter 1 around how people communicate in cyberspace; but also acknowledging the self-confidence and self-trust needed to develop and maintain an individual style and method that is congruent with our day-to-day practice as a coach offline.

Much of the anxiety around becoming a successful online coach stems from the anxiety around using technology itself, rather than trust in our communication skills. If we pause to consider how much of our daily communication is now done via text – through emails, text messaging, social networks or other communication tools – we can see how immersed our written communication skills have actually become.

There are three facets of written Internet communication that we need to be aware of up front: netiquette; use of emoticons and emojis; and the tendency to use acronyms and abbreviations. However, it is important to understand that just because these exist, we do not have to fill our messages with them. They are useful in finding the personal style of written communication which ties in with that of each individual client, and at a minimum an awareness of them prevents confusion as to what it is your client is trying to communicate to you. Framing this within the boundaries of Internet communication as a whole, you will discover a type of communication with each client that is comfortable, meaningful and fulfilling.

DOI: 10.4324/9781315685939-4

Appropriate email communication

When we sit opposite a client, our posture, facial expression, gestures and tone of voice all convey messages that either complement the words we are speaking or actually convey a message itself. In removing these, the (usually) black-on-white starkness of typed text can be startling within a coaching relationship when our training has conditioned us to work with the physical presence and its nuances. In addition, typed written communication that is easily and conveniently sent over the Internet has made us lazy with text, dropping capital letters and not worrying about misspellings and typos. Easily sent email often seemingly breaks down hierarchical barriers, allowing for a relationship that has less connotations of power between two people, such as a boss and an employee. It is likely that you have at least one example of a time when you dashed off an email to say whatever was on your mind at the time to someone with whom you would exercise more caution in a face-to-face situation.

In 2004, Suler offered an analysis of email peripherals such as username, subject line and how you greet the other party (and how you sign off), which suggested a complex anatomy of an email, including the overt communication but more interestingly how much can be read into the seemingly insignificant aspects of the communication that are full of covert meaning. This analysis looks at areas such as how the movement from a pseudonym to one's real name expresses a desire to drop masks that anonymity may afford us, and how looking at how we convey personal information through the block of text included after our sign-off (the email 'sig') is interpreted as identifying what the person holds dear to their public identity. While over-analysis of emails need not be done on a daily basis, it is important to consider such details as to what is conveyed by us in offering our professional coaching persona. Emails, mostly read on screen and skimmed rather than analysed, can be extremely emotive and yet are rarely examined as to *why* they often elicit such extremes of emotion in the wider context of our work and lives.

Netiquette

The creation of the World Wide Web (WWW) involved a dream by its creators, Tim Berners-Lee and the team at the Conseil Européen pour la Recherche Nucléaire (CERN). The dream was that it would mirror 'the ways in which we work and play and socialize' (Berners-Lee, 1998). The word 'mirror' is important here, as what actually happened was that the WWW went beyond that – it developed its own niceties and norms and, interestingly, its own particular strand of deviance and actionable wording. The rules of polite respectable behaviour online are the rules of 'netiquette', defined by Wikipedia in May (2009) as 'a colloquial portmanteau of *network etiquette* or *Internet etiquette*, [which] is a set of social conventions that facilitate interaction over networks'. Deviance from the basic rules of polite, respectful behaviour is considered poor netiquette, much as poor etiquette exists in society in the offline world.

Shea (1994) lists ten rules of netiquette, all applicable to the coaching professional working online. Many areas of Internet use when planning, setting up or delivering a service will need participation in discussions with colleagues or other professionals, and it remains important to retain polite professionalism at all times. At the very least, time spent in cyberspace will be much more pleasant for you both personally and professionally if you are aware of the rules!

Rule 1: Remember the human

It is surprisingly easy at times when sitting alone with one's device to forget that there is a human being at the other end of the communication strand! This human being deserves all the inflection and tones that you would offer them if speaking, as a method of delivering your intended meaning. Your written words may make perfect sense to you when you add tone and inflection in your head – but transferring that to the written sentence takes a level of sophistication.

Rule 2: Adhere to the same standards of behaviour online that you follow in the offline world

We live in a world – eagerly reported by the media – where online behaviour can be seen as being somehow outside society. Good examples of this are rife on Twitter, where death and rape threats are frequent and given almost in response to anything at all. It is often worth considering, well before hitting the send button, whether you would be behaving in that particular way if you were offline – so for example, if face to face with another person, would you be behaving in the same way and saying the same things?

Rule 3: Know where you are in cyberspace

Within the overall societal norm of the rules of netiquette, there are likely to be even more rules depending on the domain you are in. This could be a forum, chat room, Facebook page or LinkedIn group. Before joining any online community, checking the rules of the group and listening to the conversations taking place to get a feel for tone and content is time well spent, before jumping in with your own opinions and thoughts. With this stage of becoming part of a community, we can avoid being penalised by group facilitators or offending members of the group unintentionally.

Rule 4: Respect other people's time and bandwidth

Remember that you are not the centre of cyberspace! Inboxes are filled with unnecessary reactions to communications, and while you may agree with something that has been said, you do not have to tell everyone uninvited. Likewise, you do not have to copy everyone into an email – consider who actually needs to know the information. When developing marketing email lists, ensure the people included actually want to be there in the first place to get your information – and then double-check with them that they do (the 'double opt-in' tool). Although spam filters are more sophisticated than ever, receiving unsolicited mail remains a bugbear of us all!

Rule 5: Make yourself look good online

You will be judged by the quality of your writing in emails, forum postings and in chat rooms – that is, you will be judged by your appearance in text. Put simply, you are what you post. Platforms such as Facebook, LinkedIn and Twitter give us an opportunity to recreate ourselves in a better light online, so giving the right impression professionally is a skill we have all had to develop. This is not to indicate that we should be untruthful however, as no one appreciates being lied to. What is needed is a balance between one's congruent self and the opportunity the Internet gives us in portraying that in a good light.

Rule 6: Share expert knowledge

Where your knowledge is of use to others, share as much as possible without upsetting your bank manager! While our trainings have structure and content that took years to research and develop, and therefore need payment to have access to it, that does not mean that we do not have a lot more that we are happy to share freely. For example, our in-house magazine TILT was a quarterly publication that is offered for free online – our way of giving back to the profession.

You may also become inundated with requests for your opinion on something for free – which can become a huge time sink (something that takes a lot of your time and effort in order to be completed) and be quite exhausting. Again, this requires a balance and a positive attitude – wherever possible and time permitting – to respond politely to requests for information or opinion.

Rule 7: Help keep flame wars under control

Flame wars occur when someone has been intentionally rude or insulting and essentially wants to start a fight, or when the meaning and tone of a message have been misunderstood and reacted to. Individual messages are the 'flame' and several of them go back and forth to create the 'flame war'. These flames are fanned when the text is on the Internet for all to see and people leap to make judgements or take sides. If you are a member of a community, you are responsible for ensuring you do your part to douse the flames and maintain a pleasant environment.

Rule 8: Respect other people's privacy

You may have access to back-ups of people's personal data and messages, particularly in a work setting, but this does not give you permission to access it. Intrusion on other people's privacy also stems from knowing when they are online in certain environments, such as our 'available' status on Facebook or Google chat. In these circumstances, it is polite to check if the person is available to talk before sending uninvited instant messages (particularly if there is no real reason to do so!).

Rule 9: Do not abuse your power

In many online environments, someone is in charge! This could be the administrator of a social network group, a facilitator of a coaching group or the person who created a discussion area on LinkedIn – in each case, a facilitator will hold more power than other members to withhold messages and regulate membership. Such powers should not be abused.

Rule 10: Be forgiving of other people's mistakes

Although the Internet is primarily an unavoidable part of our daily lives and work, there will always be people who are new to specific areas of it. If you do come across an example of where someone has made a communication error due to being less familiar with the rules, be forgiving. There is no need to point out to the entire membership of the forum that they have made a mistake.

Netiquette is sometimes seen as something quirky about Internet communication, and therefore not to be taken seriously. However, since the spread of the Internet into almost all corners of our lives, it is worth giving as much thought to correct behaviour within it as we do to areas of our offline lives. In this way, as a minimum we can avoid much unpleasantness, and at a maximum create a dynamic living workspace every bit as creative and enjoyable as those we develop offline. In being a coach in practice, we often use the technique of modelling behaviour for our clients, and this must be extended to our behaviour over the Internet.

Emoticons

One of the most impressive things about the human being is their ability to develop new communication skills where previous skills are rendered obsolete in a particular environment. One of the solutions to having no physical presence when working only with the typewritten word is the use of what is known as emoticons – the creative use of keyboard characters to indicate to the other person what is happening at your end of the conversation. These emoticons have developed into what are called *emojis* – even more sophisticated renditions (small pictorial icons) of what we are feeling or doing to someone who cannot see us.

While emoticons are often seen as somehow trite, particularly in the talking professions struggling to work out how online communication could fit into our suite of how we work with another individual, they are important at times not only in conveying emotion but also in reducing the number of potential misunderstandings that can occur with the written word.

To list the many tens of thousands of emoticons that exist, particularly in such a fast-moving environment such as the Internet, would be fool-hardy. In our professional lives, we can usually get away with having an awareness of just three – the 'smiley', the 'sadface', and the 'winky'. In their most stripped back form, they are:

:) the smile, used in place of a physical smile
:(sadface, used to express feelings of sadness
;) the winky, used to indicate irony or when a joke is being made.

NetLingo.com is the most popular dictionary of Internet terms and nuances, with a vast array of emoticons available to us.

In coaching work, the use of emoticons generally needs to be led by the client. Therefore, if your coachee uses emoticons regularly as shorthand to convey what they are feeling, it can be entirely appropriate to include them in your own communications. Looking up emoticons you are unfamiliar with at sites such as Netlingo (rather than asking what they mean) is polite and means that the flow of a conversation is not interrupted. Simple use of emoticons within a session can make a big difference in containing the client and making each participant's presence felt to their correspondent. If a client smiled at you in a face-to-face situation, it is unlikely that you would fail to return that smile.

Acronyms and abbreviations

Acronyms are also widely used in cyberspace communication. The nature of written online communication, with the typed word generally taking longer than the spoken word, dictates a certain amount of truncation where possible to speed things up. In addition, there often remains a lag between a synchronous message being sent and it being received, even with powerful bandwidth being available, so anything to make the communication more expedient should be welcome. Examples of acronyms as textspeak are:

BRB   Be Right Back (to the keyboard and therefore the conversation)
LOL   Laugh Out Loud
BTW   By The Way

As with emoticons, there are many acronyms which are now ubiquitous, and some have even fallen into use as a spoken word when delivered with a certain sense of irony, such as LOL (Laugh Out Loud). Also, as with emoticons, it is the practitioner's responsibility to find the meaning of an acronym on one of the many websites that list them, before using up session time to ask for a translation.

Parents may find their children using a whole new language to maintain their privacy online, and so keeping up to date with popular acronyms and their often-fleeting use is sensible. For example, PIR is often used to indicate where a teenager or child is unable to talk freely (Parents In Room).

Enhancing text

As noted in Shea's (1994) rule 5 of netiquette – you are how you type. This can often mean intentionally making creative use of the tools at your fingertips (your keyboard) to enhance the text to imbue it with meaning, emphasis and emotion. By being creative with keyboard strokes, misunderstandings can be minimised and your voice can be heard clearly, which in turn increases the sense of you being present. It also makes for dynamic and interesting reading where the text could instead be flat and dull.

To convey oneself online, it is important to develop a personal style in order to have a congruent reflection of the self. To illustrate, the sentence that does not start with a capital letter could be read as laziness on behalf of the writer, or it could be read as indicating a softer tone of voice. In general, however, there are ten basic guidelines to enhancing text:

1 Use of capitalisation

For the most part, using capital letters in text is considered to be shouting. It can however be used to emphasise single words and can be useful in short bursts. As indicated above, a lack of use of capital letters can indicate a softer tone of voice or could simply be read as laziness, which could be disrespectful in many circumstances.

2 Emphasis

Originally, in the days before Windows and other user-friendly interfaces, the DOS text packages available contained no ability to emphasise words with bold text, underlining or italics. The convention then was to use _either_ underscores *or* asterisks to show where a word was being emphasised. This tradition remains in parts of Internet communication today.

3 Use of exclamation marks

Overuse of exclamation marks to make a sentence amusing can also make text difficult to read and irritate the recipient. A smiley or winky emoticon does a better job of indicating an exclamation, and although one or two exclamation marks are usually acceptable, an awareness that overuse can make communications flippant is wise.

4 Signature files (sig files)

Signature files are a useful tool in business and the professional use of email and can be inserted automatically by the software package being used after initial set-up by the user. Again, an awareness of the intention of the sig file can be important – they can be useful in providing a handy reference of contact details but can also look over-stern within the context of a professional, friendly, coaching email.

5 Emotional bracketing and parenthetical use

In cyberspace, it is perfectly acceptable to hug one another, often more so than in professional offline work! Hugs are given by bracketing a person's name (or screen/login name), and clients often like the session to end with a hug as it increases the sense of presence, thus:

((((Jane))))))

In addition, it is possible to give a group hug in a chatroom, thus:

(((((room)))))

Other forms of parentheses can help indicate a change in tone of voice and be useful to make text a dynamic, chatty way of communicating. For example:
    This can be a good sentence, <<but this could indicate a change in tone of voice?>>
    Or
    I try and try to change how I react to things, but rarely see any progress [[sigh]].

6 Cc'ing, bcc'ing and address books

One of the more problematic facets of working online is the ability to send one email to many people, either with everyone's knowledge (cc'ing) or not (bcc'ing). Extra care needs to be taken when hitting the 'reply' or 'reply all' buttons when working with email, as coaching client work retains a heightened sense of the confidential nature of communications.

Care is also needed when using email for client work where the email software conveniently automatically fills in the address details for us! Email addresses for two different people can often be similar, and ensuring the message gets to the right person is important.

7 Greetings and sign-offs

By their very nature, these come down to the individual practitioner's style and preference, and often change over the course of a written relationship in becoming less formal as time goes on. It is worth taking some time to develop the range of sign-offs used in particular within coaching work, where it can often leave a client feeling positive about the work they are doing with you.

8 Subject lines

Some practitioners (Chechele and Stofle, 2003) use famous inspiring quotes as the subject line to their emails. Others prefer to use the space as a strong indication that the email is confidential in nature and therefore needs special attention. In all cases, not putting a subject at all (easily overlooked) is bad practice, indicating a lack of care – although increasingly the email software being used will alert you if the subject line is absent.

9 Paragraphing and definition of the conversation

When using a narrative style for working with a client, whether by email or forum, the body should always consist of many shorter paragraphs to give the client sizeable chunks to work with, as this often helps them feel that they are managing the issues. Unbroken sections of text are difficult to read and feel chaotic and overwhelming to the client. A five-paragraph structure to an email is often a useful guideline to use, and many examples of this can be found online as well as the detail provided later here.

Some practitioners prefer to use what is called a 'living document' style of writing, where you insert text into the original document. This can create a live conversation in text, which can be powerful to read, although living document emails tend to get unwieldy after four sessions (i.e. four exchanges of the document).

10 The language of chat

Within a chat environment, we rarely have the luxury of using all the words we would in a verbal conversation! Therefore short, pithy sentences are required, not least because some chat software limits the number of characters you can use. What has been identified as essential in chat software within the context of using it professionally is that there is some indication of when the other person (or persons) is typing, which helps one sit back and wait for them to finish. Without this, different parts of the conversation can overlap and become confusing, although experienced users of chat often find it quite normal to hold many parts of chat within the same dialogue quite easily.

Many practitioners feel that there is a more intimate quality to a chat conversation compared to email conversations, which can be illustrated by thinking of an email as a letter and a chat session as a consultation room. When composing either, it is just as important to prepare your space as you would for an in-room consultation. The chances of interruption or distraction should be minimised, and the coach must prepare the coachee to do likewise in order to create a serene space in which to work during the coaching process.

As well as the various elements of netiquette to be taken into consideration, and awareness of how the lack of visual and/or auditory cues is affecting the conversation, other elements may also be impacting on the communication. This has been referred to as the 'black hole effect' by Suler (1997) and can also be applied when the client drops out of coaching entirely without notice and becomes uncontactable via their email address – as email addresses can be created on a temporary basis. A good online coach will of course have back-up communication systems in place, not least in case of technological breakdown, but client drop-out can still happen due to dissatisfaction with the technology itself rather than the skills of the coach.

Writing Letters to Clients via Email

Coaching via email is different from other digital methods of delivery as email exchanges are always asynchronous and do not occur in real time. For this reason, many coaches may be at a loss in knowing how to structure a coaching email. In determining a template for the coaching email, the authors use the five-paragraph essay as a starting point for a workable framework. This essay template is often taught in language arts education for young persons. The summary below gives an overview of the five-paragraph essay followed by the coach's five-paragraph email template.

A good introductory paragraph is organised from general to specific, states the main idea of the essay and ends with a specific thesis statement that alerts the reader to the body of the essay. The three paragraphs offer supporting information to a thesis statement, which ends the introductory paragraph. The third paragraph generally contains details supporting the thesis statement. Finally, the concluding paragraph begins specific, restating the thesis, and concludes broadly (Levin, 2004).

When considering how to structure a coaching email, the first formal work should follow initial emails that establish the coaching relationship, with an agreement and other housekeeping issues. Once the relationship is established and the introduction to the service has been completed, the coach may ask one or two powerful questions to initiate the client's initial email to the coach. Such questions as 'What brings you to coaching?' Or 'You stated in your initial query that you are hoping to achieve your wellness goals. Can you expand on that?' The client is not expected to write an email of any specific length, but a prompt requesting at least a paragraph or two is instructive and helpful.

The coach's response may follow a template such as the one the authors offer here. This is a helpful framework and is flexible. The coach may find the template aids in writing a response or may find that it stifles creative dialogue. What is paramount is that the voice of the coach is authentic. It should be noted that the standard five-paragraph essay has been critiqued as causing language arts students to become less creative, locking their writing voice into a style that should serve as a guide and not as a prescriptive process (Foley, 1989; Moss, 2002; Wesley, 2000).

Using the five-paragraph essay template, you can begin to construct a coaching email using a similar structure. A good introductory paragraph offers salutations to the client, an inquiry about the client's well-being, and ends with a statement that reflects the client's core issue. Then three supporting paragraphs make up the 'body' of your response.

The first paragraph empathises with the client and mirrors back with active listening phrases such as 'What I hear you saying is'. The second paragraph addresses what the client has done in the past, and the third offers interventions and suggestions for moving forwards. The concluding paragraph restates the core issue through mirroring and an empathic response and broadens to a general closing that sends the client into the days ahead. Following this format, your response will typically be at least 500–1,000 words.

To recap: paragraph one gives you a chance to introduce the session, thank the client for any previous correspondence and offer reassurance. In early emails, you may also like to point out that you appreciate the strength of the client in seeking guidance. This is also a good place to offer a reminder link to relevant pages on your website, such as process details or safeguarding resources.

Paragraphs two and three (or more) contain the 'meat' of your coaching email, finding focus on what appears to you to be the salient presenting topic to which the client is asking for support. Remember that your interpretation of the focus may not be the client's; so be sure to check in with them around what they wish to work on during sessions. The last paragraph before conclusion is the opportunity to call the client to action regarding the client's stated goals.

The final paragraph offers summary and closing comments. Be sure to include a few powerful, open-ended questions to clarify points, or to help the client open up in their writing.

A note on cultural issues within text

There are of course many cultural issues to consider when working with a coachee at a distance. It is the remit of the distance coach to determine whether the client's background is likely to have an impact on how the coaching process is conducted and what the likely successful outcomes could be in light of those differences if the coach does not understand or appreciate them.

As coaches, we do not need to know every single nuance of how each culture has developed its own ways of adapting sets of keystrokes to convey a thought or feeling. However, we do need to know that these different ways of communicating exist and have some awareness of what those specific differences look like when they arise if it is not to get in the way of the coaching process. Different languages create different acronyms, and so a set of letters that are ubiquitous in the English-speaking world (such as LOL) are likely to be different in, say, France where the equivalent is MDR (mort de rire – died of laughter). An added layer of nuance is considering the particular regional differences between French and French-Canadian – but a simple Google search is usually enough to pick such matters apart if they arise in written communication from your client.

Emoticons, as discussed, have developed since the days of needing to use individual keystrokes to replicate something near to a facial expression, and are frequently depicted by a small cartoonish image rather than the traditional use of ASCII text (the original code used by early computer programmers). However, there may be occasions when you are surprised by an unfamiliar set of characters within your work. This may be because your non-western client is using an emoticon which does not use the strategy of tilting one's head to read it, and the emoticon can be read as a facial representation on a straight level, such as (<_>) or Q_Q.

It is worth repeating here that we do not need to know each nuance of the cultural differences in using text to hold a conversation! Awareness of the fact that these differences exist is usually enough to work through any occurrences that appear confusing at first within the communication.

References

Anthony, K. and Nagel, D.M. (2010). *Therapy Online (A Practical Guide)*. London: Sage.

Berners-Lee, T. (1998). 'The World Wide Web: A Very Short Personal History', in *W3C World Wide Web Consortium*. www.w3.org/people/berners-lee/shorthistory.html [accessed 8 March 2021].

Chechele, P. and Stofle, G. (2003). 'Individual Therapy Online Via email and Internet Relay Chat', in S. Goss and K. Anthony (eds.), *Technology in Counselling and Psychotherapy; A Practitioner's Guide*. Basingstoke: Palgrave Macmillan.

Foley, M. (1989). 'Unteaching the Five-paragraph Essay', *Teaching English in the Two-year College*, 16(4), pp. 231–235.

Levin, P. (2004). *Write Great Essays: Reading and Writing for Undergraduates and Taught Postgraduates*. Maidenhead: Open University Press.

Moss, G. (2002). 'The Five-paragraph Theme', *The Quarterly of the National Writing Project*, 24(3), pp. 23–25, 38.

Shea, V. (1994). *Netiquette*. San Francisco: Albion Books.

Suler, J. (1997). *The Black Hole of Cyberspace (and the Unanswered Email)*. http://users.rider.edu/~suler/psycyber/blackhole.html [accessed 3 March 2021].

Suler, J. (2004). 'The Psychology of Text Relationships', in R. Kraus, J. Zack and G. Striker (eds.), *Online Counseling: A Manual for Mental Health Professionals*. London: Elsevier Academic Press.

Wesley, K. (2000). 'The Ill Effects of the Five-paragraph Theme', *The English Journal*, 90(1), pp. 57–60.

Wikipedia. (2009). 'Netiquette', *Wikipedia, The Free Encyclopaedia*. http://en.wikipedia.org/wiki/Netiquette [accessed 7 April 2009].

Chapter 4

Practical issues in coaching

Introduction

Coaching is personal. Pursuing goals and creating plans is personal – personal to self, personal to identity, personal to organisations and businesses. In coaching, what may seem like a professional endeavour may become a personal one; and what may seem to be a desire for a personal goal may occasionally rub up against personal pain.

This brings us to our role here, with coaches of all walks and definitions. Whether you are a Life Coach, Personal Coach, Personal Trainer, Business Coach, Executive Coach, Financial Coach, Career Coach, Spiritual Coach (the list is endless . . .) – *coaching involves the personal.*

For that reason, coaches should respect the coach/client relationship with the same reverence and respect of other professional relationships in which personal information is shared. Whether in-person or via distance technology, information shared between a client and a coach should be secure and confidential.

The technical and practical aspects of online coaching are comparable to the other helping professions working online. Taking therapy as an example, the purpose and goals may be different but the actual use of technology, and the importance of understanding cyberculture and your place within it, remains the same.

According to Britton (2017), an ICF-credentialed coach in the United States, coaching is worth $20 billion annually as a profession, with over a decade of coaches connecting with their clients virtually. If we include the telephone, this distance connection has existed for even more decades prior, at least since the mid-90s. Britton cites a 2017 (Sherpa) Coaching Survey indicating that 8% of coaching conversations take place by HD video, 22% by webcam, 28% by phone and 34% in person. This is in contrast to in 2008, where findings indicated 48% of coaching occurred in person and 40% by phone.

The most recent Sherpa (2020) global survey summarises that video conferencing tools now account for more coaching sessions than face-to-face meetings. In 2007, Sherpa reported the use of webcams and applications such as Skype when coaches were first starting to use this method of delivery. Between 2011 and 2012, the use of these methods dramatically increased. Now, the majority of coaches and clients use webcam coaching to some extent with a third of all coaching

DOI: 10.4324/9781315685939-5

services delivered via webcam. In 2012, only about 4% of coaching was delivered in HD – now that number has more than doubled. Large-screen, high-definition systems deliver consistently high image quality, synchronised audio and video, and real-time delivery without lags or dropouts. At large corporate firms, high-definition studios are becoming more widely available to coaches and clients. At the same time, low-definition video capability improves constantly. Life and wellness coaches in private practice are more accustomed to low-definition options; even so connection speeds are getting faster, video quality is increasing, and clients and coaches are gaining familiarity. Video coaching has increased even more significantly since 2010: from 5% to 25%. Older technologies such as telephone and email are also still being used. In fact, those numbers are not decreasing – telephone has stayed around 25% and email has levelled off between 5% and 10%. Video and other technologies account for two-thirds of coaching services and we should assume this will increase post-pandemic.

The following original summary of delivering services via technological means has been revised and updated with a focus on technology-assisted coaching.

Coaching via email and chat (text-based coaching)

Coaching via email can be compared to letter writing. The client writes a letter to the coach that is sent electronically, and the coach responds. The client may state why they are seeking coaching and name a vague or specific goal. The coach responds with a letter asking powerful questions and reflecting on what the client has written. Of course, the exact content and style of the coach's letter depend on their particular approach and orientation.

Services offered via email vary considerably. Email sessions may be arranged as a one-off session or in a package, typically between four and ten sessions. It should be noted that all emails between coach and client should be sent via encrypted channels. Put simply, encryption means that the messages are scrambled so that if the emails are intercepted, they cannot be deciphered, avoiding a breach in confidentiality. There are many ways emails are encrypted. Email correspondence can be accomplished using various encrypted platforms or products. Some products work much like regular email systems, with the same look and feel as an email received through Outlook or Gmail. Other email systems function as a web board so that each person is logging into the same site and viewing messages received. Hushmail and Protonmail are two current email products that work in a similar way to typical email programs for a nominal fee.

Some chat or messaging programmes limit how much you can type before you have to hit the send button. Without indicating you have more to say, the client may think you have finished and start typing a response only to find halfway through that another sentence has appeared in the chat screen (potentially changing the message type entirely). Style of talking also varies from practitioner to practitioner – many use short sentences in order to minimise lag. Many chat programmes indicate when the other party is typing, which is convenient.

There is a subtle difference between Internet Relay Chat (IRC) and Texting/Messaging (SMS) via your phone. Chat within a session is considered synchronous – in real time. One person chats and the other person responds, but the messages can overlap. Similarly, this can occur via phone texting. The phone is usually for shorter interventions (and only if encrypted), and chat is used for longer sessions. Both chat and texting can be asynchronous. One can send a message that the other person may not receive until a later time.

One could posit that there is a more intimate quality to the communication when delivering coaching via chat as opposed to email. While email may be compared to reading letters, the chat room may be seen as an actual virtual session room. The obvious difference between email as letter and chat as consultation room is that chat occurs synchronously while email is asynchronous. As in the offline session room, the virtual session room must be void of distractions. The coach creates an environment in which the work can take place without interruption and encourages the client to create a serene workspace as well. The difference between the face-to-face session room and the virtual session room is that the latter is co-created by the coach and the client, each in their own space yet conjoined by the chat process (Nagel, 2008). This ease of use avoids a certain formality that exists in face-to-face sessions and language use may become more casual, although rules of netiquette still apply.

As with email, netiquette must be understood within the context of a chat session. Use of emoticons, such as :), acronyms such as BRB (be right back) or OIC (Oh, I see), and emotional bracketing, such as [smiling] or [sigh] for emphasis, is as common in chat as within email. Several online dictionaries exist for definitions of Internet acronyms and text messaging, providing instant access to a resource that can be used even in the midst of a chat session. For instance, Netlingo has been dubbed 'the semantics storehouse of cyberspace'.

Most people are familiar with texting and chatting via phone, Facebook, Google chat, WhatsApp, and so on and there are many programs available. A coaching chat must be encrypted for confidentiality.

Coaching via telephone, VoIP and video

As well as seeing clients face to face, you may well already use telephone services to work with your client, and also use – or are considering using – video software to further enhance the relationship.

Telephone and other audio methods

While it is likely that you are familiar with landline telephones and mobile/cell phones, Voice over Internet Protocol (VoIP) may be less familiar to you. Again, put simply, any audio or visual media you are using through being connected to the Internet is using VoIP. Note that this chapter will use the term 'telephone' to refer to all three types of audio communication – landline, mobile/cell and VoIP.

Let us turn to the basic skills and considerations you will need to consider to be an effective telephone coach. A telephone coach will need to be competent in:

- Establishing techniques involved in developing and sustaining contact with a caller (such as making encouraging noises where appropriate and being comfortable using these sub-vocal communications to sustain interaction).
- Monitoring intonation and voice levels, with an awareness of how their voice pitch, quality, tone and accent may be experienced by the client.
- Coaches need to remember that facial expressions, gestures and body language can have an impact on how the client experiences their communication, even though they cannot actually be seen.
- Ability to identify and work with client distress.
- Ability to identify and deal with clients in difficult circumstances.
- Experienced in timing and methods of closing a session, particularly when clients are reluctant to do so.
- Comfortable with silence (a few moments of telephone silence can feel like minutes).

Now, let us consider some of the practical considerations when choosing to use the telephone:

- The communication tools MUST be adequate and confidential.
- You may want to consider a dedicated line (used exclusively for client work).
- Coaches MUST be competent and confident in technical usage.
- An undisturbed and quiet environment (for clients too) MUST be sought.
- You may want to consider a headset to minimise physical strain.
- Mobile phone use should be scrutinised (due to potential battery/signal failure, and confidentiality breaches because of their casual use).
- Clients should know cost of sessions and likely final costs, including call costs.
- The possibility of number display on bills should be ascertained.

A procedure should be established in light of the client ending the communication abruptly – emailing or texting to reschedule for example. The client's control of the situation should be respected and not invaded by an immediate call back by the coach. The client also needs to know that even if they have terminated a call, they may ring back within the contracted time and that the coach will be available to them for that allotted time.

Clients also need to be educated about the transition time they may need between termination of the session and the return to everyday life. Whereas this usually takes place quite easily in face-to-face work – for example, the time taken to travel back from the session – with telephone communication, the client is usually in their own home and it is good practice to end the session by checking with the client what their immediate plans are after the ending – this can be as simple as making a cup of tea or having a relaxing bath. The coach should also consider their own transition from the session back to their home life if working from home.

Videoconferencing

Questions to ask regarding videoconferencing and privacy concerns:

*   Who is in the room? (include AI, such as Alexa or Siri)
*   What can the client see?
*   What can you see?
*   Is the platform secure?
*   Is the session being recorded?
*   How is the camera positioned?

Now let us turn to the basic skills and considerations you will need to consider to be an effective video coach. It should be noted that while video on hand-held devices (such as mobile or cell phones) is possible, this chapter refers to using webcams and a PC/Mac.

*   Eye contact is important in suggesting whose turn it is to speak, and to ensure the client feels listened to and that the coach is engaged in the process. However, this can be difficult when working with a webcam as it is usually situated above, below or to one side of the screen. It is better practice to discuss this aspect missing from the work, although tips such as sitting back can adequately suggest eye contact.
*   Gestures can also be an important part in the process, although – depending on the strength of the connection – these can often distract from what is being said due to the screen 'jumping' or breaking up, and participants may find keeping hand gestures to a minimum helps with flow.
*   Low-quality connections may result in lip-synching being affected and sound breaking up, all of which can interrupt flow. An important point here is that minimal prompts (uh-huh? Or Mmm-hmm) may be received at the wrong point in the conversation due to delays in sound.
*   Coaches should recognise when technical interruptions – whether through a bad connection or faults in the software being used – become a block to the process of the coaching and both parties would benefit from switching to other means of communication, such as the telephone.
*   Although anecdotal positive effects of stretching boundaries that would apply in face-to- face work exist (such as a client 'arriving' at the video meeting in pyjamas after oversleeping and therefore not missing his session); boundary issues that may be particularly evident in videoconferencing should be addressed (such as clients bringing food and drink to the session).
*   A certain period of time for both parties to get used to the vagaries of videoconferencing should be allowed, as it is likely that any initial discomforts are likely to dissipate as the parties get used to each other.

- It is important that the coach's website clearly details the process and how to access it.
- Coaches should have a clear policy on what to do in the event of a technical breakdown, both pre-session and mid-session.

Simpson (2003), a worldwide expert on videoconferencing for the helping professions, offers the following practical tips for a videoconferencing service:

- As the quality of calls increases, facial expressions and tearfulness are easier to detect. It is worth investing in quality hardware and bandwidth.
- A solid colour (dark) background is best, without glare from a light, and if done with a heavy dark curtain, this can also improve sound quality.
- If using videoconferencing within an organisation, invest in training for employees.
- Block booking of session time in organisations can often dissipate the stress of the technical logistics needed to set up remote coaching systems.
- The camera should be positioned so that a balance of capturing head, shoulders and arms is contained within the picture.
- While soft lighting is often desirable to relax the client, it should not affect the quality of the picture.

Other considerations regarding videoconferencing

Be sure to use a platform that is encrypted. Skype was the obvious choice for many coaches and therapists, but keep in mind Skype has had many security and privacy issues. During the pandemic, Zoom became extremely popular. When choosing a videoconferencing platform, consider a platform that understands client privacy, whether that client is a coach client or a therapy client. While coaches do not need to be concerned with HIPAA (a privacy law in the United States to protect Patient Health Information – PHI), it is good to consider a platform that follows HIPAA standards, or the equivalent in other countries.

Virtual worlds and virtual reality

Avatar (a graphical representation of somebody in a computer graphical environment) and virtual reality are currently seeing an explosion in popularity as bandwidths increase, and software becomes more developed. In 2002, Goss and Anthony wrote:

> Whether 'avatar therapy' is to become one element of the future of counselling and psychotherapy is yet to be seen. But given the pace of developments in the field it is impossible to rule it out and those practitioners with a technological bent might do well to keep an eye open for whatever uses it may,

ultimately, be shown to have. What other innovations the technologists might have up their virtual sleeves we will have to wait and see.

(Goss and Anthony, 2002)

This same field of possibilities applies to avatar coaching. Avatar coaching is now a part of 'the future' discussed then, with coaching taking place in the Massively Multiplayer Online (MMO) online platform Second Life (SL). SL has its own currency, which begs a fascinating analysis of what coaching costs in a virtual world in relation to the traditional fiscal system.

In SL at least, communication is made by typing on a keyboard (the avatar types onto air, an invisible keyboard, to indicate that the person is typing, and text appears above the avatar's head). Confidentiality is easily breached in this case as the text may be seen by anyone standing close enough to the conversation. This can be lessened by the use of a private secure 'skybox', a private environment that is accessible only by those invited. Further enhancement of security may include the use of an encrypted chat/VoIP platform such as VSee. The combination of a skybox and the use of encrypted text and chat creates a secure form of communication.

Chatrooms that use avatars or other visuals are similar, allowing a computer-generated representation of a human being that can move around a virtual environment. These can be used for anything from simple social networking with participants simply talking to each other, to playing a multiuser game such as World of Warcraft (WoW), where users band together to defeat enemies and achieve goals within the game. More sophisticated environments created by the user within a given platform offer even more, allowing whole communities to be built, provision of software to allow virtual sex, and as mentioned some even have their own commerce, such as Second Life where the currency – which can be converted to actual currencies offline – is Linden Dollars (L$).

Omnichannel coaching

Screening the client for suitability to online work includes a determination of which method of delivery will most suit them. In turn, a coach may determine a preference for one method of delivery over another. Chechele and Stofle (2003) suggest that there seems to be a spectrum of closeness from email to chat to telephone and finally, video or in-person offline counselling. This may be a generality as more and more coaches and clients are using methods of delivery interchangeably.

Determining what method of delivery to use with your client is also based in part on your experience. If you have mostly delivered coaching in-person, that may always be your preferred method of delivery. Others have determined coaching via video to be as good and offer this method only. Purists who have been conducting online coaching for many years may opt for conducting only email sessions.

After adjusting to the idea that therapy can be delivered through technology assistance, most of us practice omni-channelling. Also referred to loosely in the profession as using blended technologies, Anthony (2015) states that the core congruent self can be present across a myriad of different platforms and types of software, including social media. Being an omnichannelled coach means you are recognisable on whatever modality, just as your physical presence achieves recognition in many environments offline.

We underestimate just how skilled we have been as a race at adapting to these new methods of communication – and what seemed to be a novel experience as we waited for the ping of, say, a new email message is now just part of our daily lives as we take our smart phones to bed for one last daily fix of being connected to each other.

Our understanding of congruence is crucial in the context of our client work, and it is vital to ensure that our true congruent self is present across the channels we use daily – and that includes our offline work.

Case vignette

This short case vignette demonstrates how one coach has incorporated technology into service delivery.

Eve and Marina

Marina (not her real name) found Eve's website, where she lists various coaching services including those via telephone, Skype and text. Marina emailed Eve for more information and Eve sent her back a welcoming email with the information she could use to make an informed decision about starting coaching with her. Eve encouraged her to get in touch if she had any additional questions.

After reading the information Eve had sent, Marina decided to book some telephone coaching with her. She wanted to increase her confidence at work. She was an editor for a magazine but although she came across as confident, she felt there was a large gap between the way she felt inside and the way she needed to be seen in such a high-profile job. Marina also wanted to be doing more writing.

After she booked her first telephone session by email, Eve sent Marina an intake form with some details for her coaching records as well as some questions she could begin pondering before the first session. Some clients like to get the ball rolling by really thinking about things beforehand while others prefer to talk it through during the intake session.

Marina had never had coaching before but was very motivated. After each session, Eve emailed over a Session Summary and Action Plan summarising the actions and steps she wanted to take each week. Marina was also welcome to email Eve for additional support between sessions. She decided to have weekly 30-minute telephone coaching sessions.

Within a few months, Marina felt she had addressed all she needed to at the time. She felt far more confident in her editorship and had been headhunted for another role which she decided to reject but it had boosted her confidence. By addressing the aspects of work she thrived on, as well as those she found more challenging, Marina was better able to handle stresses by making her workdays more balanced and supportive (delegating and working more in harmony with her own biorhythms).

Having completed the work together, Eve wished her well. A couple of years later, Eve heard from Marina again. She had emailed her after coming across an old Session Summary, saying:

Hi Eve,

I've been made redundant and my employer is providing us all with some money to put towards business coaching to help us take our next step.

I reread our Session Summaries from last time I had telephone coaching with you and would like to have more telephone coaching with you now, to help me figure out what I want to do next.

Regards, Marina

Having experienced big changes in her personal life, she wanted to have some more coaching. This time, the emphasis was different, but the process was the same. After each telephone coaching session, Eve would email her a Session Summary and Action Plan.

This time, the work together was over a shorter time span (fortnightly for 2 months), but the sessions were for an hour. Although Eve and Marina never met in person, the telephone and email contact enabled them to work well together.

With thanks to Eve Menezes Cunningham. For more information about Eve's telephone and online coaching services, please visit http://feelbettereveryday.co.uk/

References

Anthony, K. (2015). 'Cyberwork: Congruency and the Art of Omnichannelling', *BACP Counselling at Work*, Autumn issue:7. www.onlinetherapyinstitute.com/wp-content/uploads/2015/10/blog-image.png [accessed 16 February 2021].

Britton, J.J. (2017). *Effective Virtual Conversations: Engaging Digital Dialogue for Better Learning, Relationships and Results*. Sweden: Potentials Realized Media.

Chechele, P. and Stofle, G. (2003). 'Individual Therapy Online Via Email and Internet Relay Chat', in S. Goss and K. Anthony (eds.), *Technology in Counselling and Psychotherapy: A Practitioner's Guide*. New York: Palgrave Macmillan.

Goss, S. and Anthony, K. (2002). 'Virtual Counsellors – Whatever Next?', *Counselling Journal*, 13(2), pp. 14–15.

Nagel, D.M. (2008). 'Filling the Void in the Virtual Consultation Room', *Voices: The Art and Science of Psychotherapy*, 44(1), 98–101.

Sherpa. (2017). *Executive Coaching Survey: The 12th Annual Industry Review from Sherpa Coaching.* Cincinnati, OH: Sasha Corporation.

Sherpa. (2020). *Executive Coaching Survey Summary.* Cincinnati, OH: Sasha Corporation. www.sherpacoaching.com/pdf_files/2020_Executive_Coaching_Survey_EXECUTIVE_SUMMARY_FINAL.pdf [accessed 9 February 2021].

Simpson, S. (2003). *Video counselling and psychotherapy in practice.* In Technology in counselling and psychotherapy (pp. 109–128). Palgrave, London.

Chapter 5

Applying the IAC Coaching Masteries™ to online coaching

Beyond the short vignette offered in Chapter 4, the following applications of the IAC Coaching Masteries™ (International Association of Coaching, 2017) serve to demonstrate online coaching in action.

Establishing and maintaining a relationship of trust

Competency 1 as applied to online coaching was published in the IAC Voice (Nagel and Anthony, 2013).

Definition

> *Ensure a safe space and supportive relationship for personal growth, discovery, and transformation.*

Ensuring a space and a supportive relationship for personal growth, discovery and transformation online must include the technology and method of delivery. The first step in establishing and maintaining a relationship of trust begins with the coach's website or directory listing. The coach's ability to describe his or her approach is essential, as well as biography/background information that is professional, but easy to understand. Additional information can be linked, including any certifications, training or membership the coach holds. This helps establish trust and builds the potential client's confidence in the coach.

The client's confidence in the coach's ability to set out steps and instructions about how the process online will begin is important. This most likely entails a description and steps on the coach's website or other online directory listing. For example, how will the potential client first contact the coach? If the coach instructs the potential client to email, this process should be one that is secure and encrypted. This may be through an online third-party platform that the coach uses for all online communication, or it may be through an email platform such as Hushmail.com.

DOI: 10.4324/9781315685939-6

The coach may offer a Hushmail form that offers the potential client the opportunity to give the coach background and information. By offering a secure and encrypted means as an entry point to services, trust is established and the potential client will gain the sense that his or her privacy is of utmost importance, even before the coaching relationship begins.

Another approach may be that the coach prefers a telephone conversation first and may state this explicitly on the contact page. For example, this may state:

> *DeeAnna would like to speak with you confidentially about your coaching goals. Please call her at XXX.XXX.XXXX. You may leave a voice message as this phone is a secure line.*

In addition to the initial steps for contact, explaining the process of online coaching and how the coaching will be delivered is important. A coach may only deliver text-based coaching (email, chat or journal coaching for example), or may only engage in phone or video coaching. Other coaches may use a combination of session deliveries, including in-person. Delineating this information up front, so that the potential client has the opportunity to determine if the coach's approach fits his or her needs, can be very reassuring. If the coach's various tech deliveries offer the client choices in how the process will take place, this also aids in establishing a supportive relationship. For example, offering a questionnaire that the potential client will fill out prior to the first session could ask a question about the client's preference for coach delivery:

> *Are you interested in in-person or online coaching or both?*
> *What is your preferred online mode of communication, email, chat, audio, or video?*

Once the coaching relationship is contracted, the coach can offer guidelines for issues related to possible technological breakdown and how to re-establish contact should a break-down occur. For example, a video session may suddenly end, and unless the coach has explained the guidelines to the client, the client may not know the end of the session was not intentional. Informing the client of similar guidelines about the use of email or journal entries is also important. The following statements are examples:

> *Please know that I will never disconnect during a session with you on purpose. Should we become disconnected during a chat or video session online, try to re-establish a connection. If that is not possible, email, text, or phone me to reschedule.*

OR

> *I will always respond to your emails within three business days. If you have sent an email and you do not receive a timely response, please do not hesitate to send a follow-up email.*

OR

> *Your journal entries are a vital part of your growth process. Should you send me journal entries between our scheduled sessions, or in between email exchanges, know that I may not have the opportunity to reply to each journal entry. When we meet again (or when I email a formal reply) I will ask if there is a particular journal entry that you would like me to review and offer feedback.*

Another key element in establishing a safe environment when working online is to discuss the Online Disinhibition Effect (see Chapter 7). This can be accomplished very simply by explaining to a new client that working online often has positive rewards as we tend to be able to open up easily. Encourage the client to become aware of his or her comfort level as they disclose information. For example:

> *You may find that working online works for you because some people find it is easier to be open and honest about the coaching process – how you are progressing on your goals or what seems to be difficult. We have time, so be sure to check in with yourself about how much you are disclosing. It is easier to open up but sometimes when we share too much too quickly, we might feel a bit vulnerable afterwards. If this happens, feel free to talk to me about it.*

Because of disinhibition, establishing 'between session' strategies is important. One example that we have already referred to is journal writing. Keeping the client engaged between sessions can aid in the client feeling safe, resulting in the client taking more risks in the coaching relationship. Other examples of 'between session' strategies may include sending a positive affirmation text or emailing an article of interest to the client.

  With regard to online communication, pacing and cues are different. Educating the client about the nuances of online conversation may be necessary and can also give the client a feeling of security knowing that the coach is willing to teach him or her about the unique aspects of the communication. For example, during a chat session, the coach might write:

> *When you are typing out your thoughts, take your time. You can send me bits of information at a time by simply entering after you have typed a sentence or two. Likewise, I will do the same. If you ask me a question and I am pausing to think, I will type [pausing] to let you know that I am with you, but I am contemplating your question.*

OR

> *Sometimes during an audio or video session, depending on our connections, we may hear an echo, or one or both of us may experience lag. And sometime eye contact may seem different than being in an in-person session. If you*

have an external video camera, feel free to adjust the camera to best suit your view.

Perceiving, affirming and expanding the client's potential

Definition

> *Recognises and helps the client acknowledge and appreciate his or her strengths and potential.*

If the client appears hesitant about the use of technology, becoming accustomed to the platform the two of you will be using through a simple and effective introduction can be helpful. You can create a simple 'How to' page on your website or direct the client to a video tutorial if available. This is not much different than a client seeing you in person for the first time, hesitant to make that initial contact. This step has the effect of the client having a greater appreciation of personal capabilities and potential within the coaching relationship and expanding that confidence and potential beyond.

Key elements of this mastery include being empathetic with the client. In using the written word via chat or email, the coach may use the following sentence in the initial session or email to describe an empathic understanding:

> *It sounds as if you are struggling with X (e.g. time management) but I can hear your determination to move forward.*

Distinctions in the coaching relationship mean that the use of language, both verbal and written, must be intentional and articulate to ensure that the words reflect believing versus judging, enabling versus pushing, and expanding versus stretching. Often in textual online coaching, the verbatim transcript is available for coach and client to access after the session; therefore, the accurate use of the written word is essential.

> *One way to practice the use of the written word effectively is to record a live in-person session and transcribe that session. Review and study the transcript for the proper use and intent of the words. If you were to have conducted the session online without aural or visual cues would you have used different words to convey the meaning?*

Sample effective behaviours include connecting the client's potential with possible opportunities and resources within the client's organisation (if applicable). The coach can ensure that the client knows about additional online or intranet resources that may assist them.

Sample ineffective behaviours include cheerleading or using exaggerated or insincere enthusiasm. In online coaching, when using chat rooms or asynchronous communication, an example would be the overuse of emoticons or abbreviations. Another ineffective behaviour is described as accepting, rather than being curious about, the client's perceived assumptions, limitations and obstacles. Using simple phrases either verbally or via the written word can include phrases such as 'I am wondering if'.

Creating or encouraging client dependency is also ineffective. When a coach offers online coaching, this can often be a way to offer services as an adjunct to in-person coaching or stand-alone. As online sessions are sometimes easier to access, due to lack of travel time to an office and more convenient scheduling, creating a step-down coaching schedule can be effective. For example, 30-minute video, phone or chat sessions can be effective as a step-down from full hour sessions. Email sessions (a session equals one full exchange between client and coach) can be arranged every other week as the coaching relationship winds down.

Measures of this mastery include the coach encouraging more action from the client beyond the client's previous comfort zone, motivating the client to complete assignments, and the client becoming more aware of behaviours.

The coach can lead the client to more action by offering written assignments and online or app-related assignments. An incentive for the client to be inspired to complete the assignments could be that the client can send the assignment to the coach 'between sessions' instead of waiting until the next in-person meeting time. If the client has the ability to reach out to the coach between sessions with completed materials or thoughts towards a goal, this can affirm and expand the client's potential. Being sure to check in with the client regarding the translation of the assignment to real-world application is also essential.

Engaged listening

Definition

> Gives full attention to the words, nuances and unspoken meaning of the client's communication, the coach is more deeply aware of the client, his/her concerns, and the source of the issue, by listening beyond what the client is able to articulate.

Key elements of this mastery include the coach listening beyond what the client articulates. This is necessary in textual communication too – to be able to 'listen' beyond the client's written words. This is also referred to as the latent versus manifest content. To hear the latent meaning in dialogue requires a consultant, coach or manager to listen at times with an 'analytic ear'; that is, to listen to what is being said in a state of suspended attention rather than with the usual focused attention we give to those to whom we are talking. All conversations can be read for its manifest and latent content. At times, the latent content is more significant than the intended communication. This also helps to identify the 'core issue' the client may be bringing to you, but not necessarily identifying it as such.

An example of this may be a client who is reaching out to a coach to work on motivation to complete a project. This is what the client discusses with you during conversations, online or in-person. During the time you work with the client you discover, through the client's self-report and through demonstration of late submission of assignments, that your client has a pattern of not completing or being late with the projects within a project. You determine that it may be helpful to work on the larger topic of motivation and procrastination rather than just applying your coaching to the current project at hand; or you may determine to accomplish both simultaneously, using the current project as an example of how the client can work on future projects as well. This is accomplished by listening to the latent and the manifest content within the dialogues.

Sample effective behaviours include using nominal cues to give the client the opportunity to reflect or respond, and this can be achieved textually in a chat by first observing whether or not the client is typing a response. Most chat programs give an indication when the other person is typing. You can further offer support by typing phrases such as 'take your time'. You can encourage clients to enter the typed response every few sentences so that you can be reading the response as the person continues typing the complete thought. In asynchronous communication such as email, both the coach and the client have an opportunity to reflect due to the nature of the correspondence.

Another sample effective behaviour is noticing nuances in the client's communications. More misspelled words than usual may indicate the client is feeling rushed or is distracted for example. Confirming a client's communications might include the coach reflecting through the written word or verbally:

> *What I hear you saying is . . .*
> *It sounds like . . .*
> *Correct me if I am misunderstanding . . .*

In addition, with textual communication, the listening may continue between sessions as the coach has the opportunity in most cases to review the verbatim transcripts of the session.

Effective behaviours also include discerning the appropriate coaching method to use based on the client's needs and concerns, and this also translates to discerning the appropriate methods of delivery. For example, more preparation is needed on the part of the coach and the client if the method of delivery begins online and transitions to in-person due to the disinhibition effect; yet moving a client from in-person to online or phone is much less difficult and can be used effectively to accommodate the client's needs or scheduling constraints. This is also an indication that the coach understands the mastery by adapting the coaching methodology and strategy, as necessary, for the client.

An example of ineffective behaviour includes missing the client's deeper points in the communication (this may include the latent content). When using multimedia approaches such as webinar platforms or video platforms, client communication can be missed as the coach multitasks, for example listening, typing in the chat area and paying attention to multiple conversations during a group session. In addition, as the progression of the conversation is not linear, communicating in a chat room requires constant eye scrolling both up and down.

One **measure of effectiveness** is noting that the client's tone and flow of ideas become more open and effortless. This is evidenced in email as the client's asynchronous exchanges become more fluent and narrative, rather than simply answering previous questions, or clarifying for the coach. The client's story (manifest and latent) begins to emerge.

As mentioned in the mastery guide, a common mistake is thinking the coach has to speak when the client is quiet. This silence may come across differently on the phone as opposed to in a chat room or video, so coach awareness of the varying nuances in the different methods of technology delivery is important. For example, silence may mean that the client has not responded for a while (perhaps a week or two have passed) and setting a protocol for sending an alert to the client can be important. An example follows:

Hi Mary,

How are you? I am checking in as I have not heard from you in a couple of weeks. I just wanted to let you know that I will be closing the file in a week or so assuming you feel you have accomplished your goals. However, I would love for us to continue as I think we could accomplish a bit more. If you would like to proceed, just send me an email in the next few days.

Warm regards, Coach

Processing in the present

Definition

> *Focus full attention on the client, processing information at the level of the mind, body, heart and/or spirit, as appropriate. The coach expands the client's awareness of how to experience thoughts and issues on these various levels, when and as appropriate. The coach uses what is happening in the session itself (client's behaviour, patterns, emotions, the relationship between the coach and the client) to assist the client toward greater self-awareness and positive appropriate action.*

This has the **effect** of the client being able to express and engage with present reality. Depending on the cues available, the coach can monitor the client's affect to be sure that they are staying in the present, not just within the conversation but with mannerisms that are congruent as well. If the coach and client are communicating via written communication, the coach will use empathic mirroring and listening skills beyond what is typical in an audible conversation by checking in with the client, using clarifying statements such as '*I hear you saying. . .*'

Key elements include the coach being aware of the dynamics occurring within the session, both within the client and between coach and client, and understanding how the dynamics are affecting the client and the coaching. The coach also has the ability to discern past from present in the client's dialogue and has a simultaneous and holistic awareness of their communications at all levels. This involves listening with a 'third ear' or using one's 'sixth sense' or seeing with the 'mind's eye'. When paralinguistic and/or audible cues are removed from the communication process, we tend to rely more on our instincts or intuition.

The coach can guide the client as the client remains in tune with his or her body in the present. The client may also be aware on a visceral level what effect written words or the online experience (particularly in a virtual world setting) is having so that the client is paying attention to gut reactions and conveying this to the coach. This becomes an **effective behaviour** for the coach, who checks in with the client about thoughts, feelings and intuition and what the client is feeling in his or her body as appropriate.

Another important factor specifically related to the online session is to be sure that the client and the coach have prepared the space for the coaching session. Being aware of distractions that may lead one or both off focus and being aware of possible distractions such as deliveries or tradespeople working outside is crucial. Closing all other browser windows so that neither is distracted by pings from others on social media is important. Encouraging the client to explore different levels of knowing outside the session may be beneficial, for example experimenting in a virtual world or online gaming environment; writing down thoughts in an online journal writing platform or joining a support group or discussion forum. Encouraging the client to explore his or her own inner knowing can be part of exploring different levels of knowing within cyberspace. The coach who can 'hear' the deeper levels of the client's story can guide the client towards a reached goal.

It is also important to realise that in the present, when using technology, if the connection is slow and there is lag time in a video session, this is the reality of using technology and the inherent glitches are not part of the coaching process exclusively. Continuing the communication despite the glitches or deciding to reschedule is part of being focused and attuned.

Distinctions include being in the here and now versus past or future, and coaches can pay particular attention to this with regard to client email responses. For example, if a client is writing a long narrative about historical issues or wishing for what might be in the future, this is a clue for the coach to redirect the client. Redirection with a client's journal writing, so that the client remains in the present with the writing experience, is to ask the client to reflect on the following after writing a particularly long entry that focuses on the past or the future:

I was: Surprised by . . .
Aware of . . .
Curious about . . .
I noticed . . .
I felt . . .

Expressing

Definition

Attention and awareness as to how the coach communicates commitment, direction, intent, and ideas – and the effectiveness of this communication.

This mastery has the **effect** of the coaching interaction being enhanced, with the client being at ease and trusting. A key element for this is for the coach to be client focused. The coach has an opportunity to offer client-focused attention by meeting the client 'where they are at' – and in the case of online coaching, this includes both accommodating the client's time and schedule and meeting the client in session with a method of delivery that suits them. Meeting the client 'where they are at' also includes the coach's use of online language and netiquette skills so that the client feels understood in a way that allows the coach to maintain a professional online presence with appropriate online boundaries.

Distinctions include how the coach conveys support and encouragement when using word alone for expression. In textual communication, this can be accomplished by using two effective strategies. The first, *descriptive immediacy*, allows the client to know what you are thinking. For example, if the client says, 'I had a really good day yesterday at work! I met my deadline!', the coach might respond with, 'I imagine a big smile on your face right now'.

Another strategy is to use what is referred to as *emotional bracketing*. Using the same client statement, the coach can convey his/her own emotion by simply responding with [smiling . . .]. While some chat programs also allow for the use of emoticons, writing the words either in the descriptive immediacy format or in the emotional bracketing format can have a more meaningful impact. This is due to the overuse of emoticons in more casual online conversation.

Building and maintaining rapport through tailored communications is a **sample effective behaviour** that can be achieved online. The coach must be aware of timing in online communication; in asynchronous communication, this may include attention to between-session emails or emails that depart from the coach dialogue. Responding to the emails appropriately without alienating the client is important. For example, within the context of the face-to-face coach relationship, should the client email between sessions with an idea or with the desire to share an 'aha' moment, the coach can acknowledge without the client expecting the online dialogue will continue. If the coach has not already established an expectation with the client via the informed consent process (e.g. 'You may email me between sessions at any time, but I may not always have the opportunity to read your emails or respond' then a simple reply such as, 'Thank you for sharing Mary! I look forward to discussing this with you in our next scheduled session. . .' serves to illustrate warmth and caring while maintaining professional boundaries.

Another effective way to demonstrate rapport through tailored communications is by accommodating the client through technology. As discussed previously, some clients may need to cancel an appointment due to scheduling or transportation issues. Or perhaps the client is on vacation but does not want to miss a session. Arranging for an online session can assist with ongoing continuity and building rapport. In addition, depending on how fees are structured, a coach may be able to tailor varying methods of delivery for a client who is dealing with financial hardship – arranging for phone sessions bi-monthly with one or two email exchanges (generally priced at a lower fee per exchange than a full-on hour session) between phone sessions.

A common mistake made by coaches includes jumping in with too many questions, even if well-intentioned. This can also occur in an email dialogue, whereby the coach asks too many questions and does not reply with a narrative about what the client has previously presented. While it may be necessary to ask clarifying questions in response to a first email exchange with the client, additional responses from the coach should include more narrative reflections and suggestions than questions.

Indicators that the coach understands this includes proper pacing within technology-delivered services. Tuning into the technological aspects of voice and video is important and maintaining a demeanour that is self-assured can be helpful in the event of technology glitches, such as the sound breaking up or video delay. The coach can take the lead in reassurance in such cases, particularly if the technology glitches repeat in each session. For example, if the coach is using video to communicate with a client in another country, there may always be a lag. Timing responses that take lag into account can help with the pacing of silent moments and conversation.

Clarifying

Definition

> *Reduce/eliminate confusion or uncertainty increase understanding and confidence of the client.*

This mastery demonstrates to the client that not only do you hear their concerns and ask clarifying questions but that you also ask the right clarifying questions at the appropriate junctures within the online sessions. As stated previously, asking too many questions (particularly in an email response) can end up resulting in the client simply answering questions instead of weaving their own interpretations and additional narrative (the story the client brings to the session) into their reply. The coach's ability to home in on the 'core issue' is paramount and must be accomplished amidst the technological nuances that exist within online coach delivery (glitches, pacing, proper use of emoticons, netiquette, and effective use of textual language). The following statements are examples of ways to clarify:

> *What I hear you saying is . . .*
> *It sounds like . . .*
> *Correct me if I am misunderstanding . . .*

If you detect an overarching theme, this may be the clue to determining the core issue. A clarifying statement in this regard may be, 'I understand that you are wanting to accomplish A, but I am wondering, since you have reported X, Y, Z, if we can take a look at B'. Asking for the client's feedback reinforces your desire for clarity with the client, for example 'What do you think about that?'

As previously noted, in online communication, there may be access to the verbatim transcript which can serve the coach in ensuring that fewer client statements were missed or ignored. With verbatim transcripts such as email and chat, the coach can revisit a statement the client made if in the initial session they missed an opportunity with the client.

A sample **effective behaviour** is connecting to something the client already knows or has experienced. One way to accomplish this is to simply ask, particularly in an initial email as the coach establishes rapport and attempts to clarify the core issue, 'If you have reached this goal or a similar goal in the past, how did you do it? What worked (or did not)?' This gives the client an opportunity to tell you more. You might also inquire about the client's support system, 'Who is most supportive to you as you work toward this goal?' This will give the coach more information about whether or not the client is supported, and if their goal is realistic.

Common mistakes include thinking the coach knows the right answers or what is best for the client. The client is less likely to think the coach is telling the client what to do if the client is adding in occasional questions such as 'Does that seem like something you could do in the next week?' or 'What are other ideas you might have?'

Helping the client set and keep clear intentions

Definition

> *Helps the client become or remain focused and working toward intended goals.*

In addition to helping the client to become or remain focused and working towards the intended goals that the client has brought to the coaching relationship, the coach can also weave the appropriate use of technology into the client's 'plan'. Accommodating the client via technology is important but establishing a clear plan for the use of technology is equally important, and helps the client stay on task with clear expectations regarding the coach/client relationship.

This is most effectively established through informed consent – both through the written informed consent agreement and through other ways that a client becomes informed about the work. For example, the coach can clearly state on his or her website, and in the written informed consent agreement, how the work will take place. An example may be:

> . . . *I see clients in-office and online. I use the jigsaw box platform which allows me to post information for you to review (articles, videos, and podcasts) and gives us a secure and confidential area to discuss your impressions.*
>
> *If you need to reach me between assignments for housekeeping issues, I use Hushmail, a secure and confidential email service. If you are travelling or not able to access our standard communication methods, we can arrange for a telephone session . . .*

This offers the client a solid foundation for the work by establishing boundaries and a contained process for communication, goal setting and goal attainment.

Another important element in ushering a client to intended goals is understanding their 'online identity'. A competent online coach understands the impact cyberspace may have on people's lives and strives to support the client's efforts within the context of cyberculture as well as in the offline world. If the coach is uninformed, or misinformed, about cyberculture, the coach may inadvertently lead the client towards goals that are incongruent with the client's cultural identity online.

For example, a coach and client may have established regular in-person or phone contact for a session. The coach may have additional assignments between sessions for the client to complete. Rather than point the client to an online method for completing the task, the coach states, 'I will mail the assignments to you so that you can complete them in the next two weeks and mail them back'. While the assignment content may be perfectly appropriate to the client's intended goals, if the client has a strong online presence and uses cyberspace for work and leisure activities, the mere action of mailing the assignments to the client may be off-putting. A writer or an editor may be more inclined to discuss goals with a coach using email coaching as this readily draws on the writer's natural abilities and talent. A busy executive who travels a lot may welcome a flexible coach who can switch between methods of delivery, from phone to email, as necessary.

Another **example** illustrates the vast opportunities in cyberspace that the coach may not be aware of or is hesitant to engage in. Perhaps a client has the goal of a new position at another company and is seeking a career coach for the purposes of updating his or her resume and gaining stronger interviewing skills. He is an illustrator, and likes his job within the comic book industry, but he would like to explore possibilities in the gaming industry. While coach and client see each other online via video sessions, the mock interviews they conduct in these sessions leave the coach and the client feeling flat. The client might be better served to engage in mock interviews within a 3D virtual world using avatars, as research has demonstrated that skills learned in a virtual world are transferable to the real world, sometimes more so than if the client learned the skills in the real world. The client may not have had the expectation that coaching services would be conducted in a 3D virtual world setting, but if the coach is aware of the possibilities for coaching within a virtual world, the client may feel more congruence in the coaching relationship and expand possibilities such as learning interview skills in a simulated virtual world.

Inviting possibility

Definition

> *Creating an environment that allows ideas, options, and opportunities to emerge.*

This mastery has the **effect** of the coach helping the client transcend barriers and offers more options.

When we think of online coaching as a way for the coach to offer more options for meeting with clients, we see immediately that opening the coaching relationship up to online delivery and technological tools achieves this. We can also see that if the client, for whatever reason, has barriers to accessing in-person coach sessions, offering online sessions can be a way to bridge that gap.

Even if the coach initially states that he or she is only interested in in-person sessions or phone sessions, the coach can let the client know that other options are available. When the client misses an appointment due to travel or traffic or even illness, online coaching can prevent the loss of momentum in the coach-client relationship.

This has the **distinction** of being creative versus prescriptive. Prescriptive indicates a set time every week in the office while the clock ticks for 50–60 minutes. Creative indicates the possibility of a 30-minute chat session twice a week, or a one-hour video session twice a month with an email exchange in between. Creative means your client keeps an online journal, or an online vision board, and invites you to read or view so that the two of you can discuss these further in the next session. Creative suggests that you might text your client a positive affirmation in between sessions to affirm a desired goal.

Sample effective behaviours include using appropriate tools and techniques to create an environment for expansion, inviting opportunity. The use of technology, not just in the delivery of the coach session, but as a tool in personal growth can enhance the client's progress and the coach-client relationship. Offering tools that move the client quicker towards goals has the effect of the client's awareness being expanded. With a plethora of apps for everything, from meditation to to-do lists, and with websites ranging from self-help and self-motivation to journaling and the creation of vision boards, the client's possibilities are expanded and opened. Even the use of Pinterest can encourage individual expression and the thoughtful emergence of ideas.

Additionally, the coach who uses a variety of techniques or coach modalities has the opportunity for horizons to expand through utilising technology. For example, we might say that narrative coaching is a modality that draws on the client's various scenarios, circumstances and cultures to expand options, demonstrating **effective behaviours**. Narrative coaching is one approach to coaching, and as with narrative therapy, the modality is particularly well-suited for the exchange of emails or 'letters' that elicit the story from the client and feedback from the coach.

Helping the client to create and use support systems and structures

Definition

> *Helping the client identify and build the relationships, tools, systems, and structures he or she needs to advance and sustain progress.*

Key elements include the coach suggesting possible support systems and structures appropriate to the client's needs. This may include a proper search of the Internet for local in-person support, meetings or networking groups that may aid the client, or online support – meetings or networking groups that may serve the same purpose. Social media may be a way for the client to reach out beyond the local community if necessary, joining groups on LinkedIn, Facebook and other relevant online networks. The client may also benefit from enhancing his/her own online presence, whether for professional or personal endeavours. This may involve teaching the client social networking skills or enhancing the client's Internet search skills and, depending on the client's Internet experience, additional education may be necessary regarding netiquette. The coach can serve as a model for the client regarding appropriate use of the Internet for networking and social/professional support.

Sample ineffective behaviours include the coach recommending resources, structures or systems without first identifying the individual client's needs. Examples of this may be suggesting the client join specific LinkedIn groups with a focus on career advancement when the client has not identified this as a desired goal but instead would like to network with like-minded people in his/her profession. This requires the coach to listen and clarify to be sure he/she is guiding the client in the right direction and is focused on the client's core issue as the Internet is vast. Without narrowing choices for the client and assisting the client with a proper Internet search, the client may feel overwhelmed. At the same time, the coach must be careful not to 'take over' and allow the client to seek resources on the Internet independent of the coach. The coach can continue building rapport by being available between sessions to help should the client become 'stuck', resulting in an Internet search that leaves the client lacking in resources.

The coach must be aware of the balance between giving the client resources and helping the client find resources; otherwise, the coach risks making the common mistake of identifying all (or most of) the actions and systems, rather than involving the client.

One **indicator** that the coach understands the mastery is addressing any inner conflict that might interfere with sustainability. For example, if the client is reticent to disclose in online groups, validating the client's fear is important. This fear may be due to a lack of experience on the Internet or may be because the client does not readily share with others online or face-to-face. When offering online support groups or mastermind groups to clients online, it is paramount for the coach to discuss with the client that some online groups are open, others may be password protected only and not encrypted, with the most secure communication online being in a group or cohort that communicates within an encrypted environment online.

References

The Coaching Masteries™ IAC. (2017). https://certifiedcoach.org/certification-anddevelopment/the-coaching-masteries/ [accessed 8 March 2021].

Nagel, D. and Anthony, K. (2013). 'Adapting the Masteries to Best Practices Established in the Delivery of Coaching Services Online: Mastery 1', *VOICE* (October). International Association of Coaching.

Chapter 6

Ethical framework for technology-delivered coaching

Introduction

The Ethical Framework for the Use of Technology in Coaching was originally published in 2011 (Labardee *et al.*, 2011) and summarised that same year in the BACP's *Coaching Today* journal (Anthony and Nagel, 2012). The framework was modelled after The Ethical Framework for the Use of Technology in Mental Health (Anthony and Nagel, 2010). Prior to the writing of the initial framework, a review of the relevant literature to date (Goss, 2011) did not reveal any research or writings regarding the ethics of online coaching.

In 2019, the framework was updated and published as a white paper (Nagel *et al.*, 2019). This revised framework was featured in summarised form again in BACP's Coaching Today journal (Anthony *et al.*, 2020).

Technology changes happen rapidly. Knowing that more and more coaches are using technology to deliver services (Kanatouri, 2020), this updated framework was both timely and necessary. Professional coaching organisations create and update codes of ethics, but to date these have not yet incorporated the use of technology into the codes and guidelines to reflect best practice. This ethical framework is offered as a point of reference for governing bodies, certifying organisations and the professional coaches these bodies and organisations represent.

The framework

A competent coach working online will always adhere to the following minimum standards and practices in order to be considered to be working in an ethical manner.

Coaches have a sufficient understanding of technology

Coaches who choose to deliver coaching services via technology will possess at least a basic understanding of technology as it relates to delivery of services, including but not limited to:

- Encryption: Coaches understand how to access encrypted services to store records and deliver communication.

DOI: 10.4324/9781315685939-7

- Password Protection: Coaches take further steps to ensure the confidentiality of coaching communication and other materials by password protecting the computer, drives, stored files or communication websites.
- Firewalls: Coaches utilise firewall protection externally or through web-based programs.
- Virus Protection: Coaches protect work computers from viruses that can be received from or transmitted to others, including clients.
- Backup Systems: Records and data that are stored on the coach's hard drive are backed up either to an external drive or remotely via the Cloud.
- Hardware: Coaches understand the basic running platform of their work computer and know whether or not a client's hardware/platform is compatible with any communication programmes the coach uses.
- Software: Coaches know how to download and operate software and assist clients with the same when necessary for the delivery of services.
- Third-party services: Coaches only utilise third-party services that offer an address and phone number so that contact is possible via means other than email. This offers a modicum of trust in the third party utilised for such services as backup, storage, virus protection and communication.

Coaches using technology will make every effort to ensure the protection of their clients' privacy and confidentiality

This includes but is not limited to:

- Coaches will use email services which provide encryption and encourage their clients to do so.
- Coaches conducting their practice over the phone will use a system that reduces the chance of being overheard, that is, land lines over cell phones; or encrypted VoIP.
- Coaches will investigate the privacy policies of any chat or instant messenger programme they may use with their clients and avoid those which do not protect confidentiality.
- Records storage can be hosted on a secure server with a third party, stored on the coach's hard drive utilising encrypted folders or stored on an external drive that is safely stored.

Coaches display pertinent and necessary information on websites

Websites provide access to information for the general public, potential clients, clients and other professionals.

- **Coach Contact Information**: Coaches offer contact information that includes email, postal address and a telephone or VOIP number. While it is not recommended that postal addresses reflect the coach's home location, clients should have a postal address for formal correspondence related to redress, subpoenas or other mailings requiring a signature of receipt. Coaches state the amount of time an individual may wait for a reply to email or voice-mail. Best practice indicates a maximum of two business days for enquiries.

- **Coach Education**: Coaches list degrees, licenses and/or certifications and, wherever possible, links supporting independent verification of certification and/or membership in a related professional organisation should be provided. Coaches consider listing other formal education such as college or university courses, online CE and professional development courses and conference/convention attendance related to coaching and technology.
- **Terms of Use and Privacy Policy:** The Terms of Use agreement and Privacy Policy documents are posted by the provider of the website and appear on websites used by the coach to promote and/or deliver coaching services. These documents outline what the user of the website and associated services may expect with respect to the availability of the website and related web services, and how private information is collected, stored and protected. Coaches using a web-based coaching platform (website), or web service provided by a third-party provider, will ensure that the Privacy Policy conforms to the privacy practice standards that the coach is held to by the professional association or governing agencies operating within the geographic region in which coaching services are provided.
- The Terms of Use agreement often appears in the footer of a website's homepage and outlines the conditions under which the provider of the website makes the site (not professional coaching services) available. The agreement is between the provider of the website (which may not be the coach) and the users of the website. It specifies what is expected with respect to the website provider's provision of website availability and security, and the website user's respect of and adherence to site policies regarding posting information and use of copyrighted or trademarked information and links to third-party websites. It often incudes a warranty and disclaimer regarding availability of the website.
- The **Privacy Policy** often appears in the footer of a website's homepage and outlines how the provider of the website, and the coach who may be using the website or web services to communicate with the client, collects and protects personal information. It defines what type of personal information is collected, how it is collected, what is done with the information, how this is protected (encrypted), how it is managed by those engaged by the provider of the website service, what the user of the website service can do to protect personal information and who to contact regarding concerns about personal information. It also addresses, if applicable, how payments are securely processed, and it should conform to the widely accepted standards that are in place within the geographic area where services are provided (such as the Fair Information Practice Principles in the United States and the General Data Protection Regulation [GDPR- 2018] in the United Kingdom and Europe).

- Coaches must also be cognisant of laws regulating professional practices within their geographic jurisdiction, and in particular, the standards and practices governing how records are maintained and what privacy and security rules may apply. In some instances, a coach may also be a health care provider by way of employment, education, certification and/or licensure. A circumstance may arise in which a government-regulated license or certification may supersede the role of coach, in effect rendering the coach a health care provider. If that circumstance arises, the coach may need to follow pertinent laws and practice standards governing the use and disclosure of protected health information. This could be those applying to US health care providers under the Health Insurance Portability and Accountability Act (HIPAA) provisions as outlined by the Health Information Technology for Economic and Clinical Health (HITECH) act.
- **Crisis Intervention Information**: People may surf the Internet seeking immediate help and may misunderstand the kinds of services a coach provides. Coaches should provide a clear explanation as to the limitations of services provided and display crisis intervention information on the home page. Offering global resources such as Befriender's International or The Samaritans is the best course of action.
- Information concerning the nature of the professional coaching services provided by the coach to the client should be provided in a separate Coaching Agreement document which is then executed as a contract for coaching services. In addition, the Terms of Use agreement should reference an associated (separate) Privacy Policy, to specify how personal information transmitted through the website is protected

Coaches work only within their scope of practice

Scope of Practice indicates the specific area to which a coach may practice:

- Coaches should have a professional affiliation which offers a code of ethics with which they comply.
- Coaches will always follow local and regional laws and ethical codes, as applicable.
- Coaches will accurately identify their coaching qualifications, expertise, training, experience, certifications and credentials.
- Coaches will maintain a reasonable level of awareness of current best business practices and professional information in their fields of activity and undertake ongoing efforts to maintain competence in the skills they use.
- Coaches understand and clearly communicate the distinction between coaching, consulting, psychotherapy and other support professionals.
- Coaches understand and adhere to a responsibility to refer clients to other support professionals when indicated.

- Coaches will encourage their clients or sponsors to make a change if the coach believes the client or sponsor would be better served by another coach or by another resource.
- Coaches do not attempt to maintain simultaneous counselling and coaching relationships with clients even when properly qualified as a coach and licensed in another profession such as counselling.
- Coaches adhere to professional codes of conduct as published by internationally recognised professional coaching organisations.
- Coaches will recognise and honour the efforts and contributions of others and not misrepresent them as their own. Coaches understand that violating this standard may leave them subject to legal remedy by a third party.
- Coaches respect the specific laws of a potential client's geographic location. While coaching may not be a regulated field where the coach is located, coaching may be (or become) regulated in other parts of the world.
- Coaches will clearly spell out any limitations on confidentiality, as defined by the applicable Code of Ethics, state or geographical jurisdiction under which they practice on their website, within their Coaching Agreement and so on.

Coaches enter into a contractual agreement with the client to provide coaching services

Coaches will carefully review the Coaching Agreement with the client, and will strive to ensure that prior to or at the initial meeting, their client and his/her sponsors understand the nature of coaching, the nature and limits of confidentiality, financial arrangements and any other terms including how coaching information will be exchanged among coach, client and sponsor (the person contacting on behalf of and paying for coaching). The coach or coaching organisation will have the client sign the Coaching Agreement or Contract, and thereby enter into an agreement for coaching before proceeding.

Coaching agreement

The process begins when the client contemplates accessing services. Therefore, clear and precise information concerning the nature of the coaching services proposed and how information is managed should be accessible via a document posted on the coach's website. The information in the Coaching Agreement includes:

- A clear description of coaching, which should include disclaimers as to what coaching is not (i.e. a substitute for therapy, legal advice).
- How web-enabled and associated telephonic and face-to-face coaching services, as available, will be provided and supported.
- A review of the pros and cons of online coaching, including such disadvantages as lack of visual and auditory cues, the limitations of confidentiality via

technology and so on; and advantages, which include easy scheduling, time management and the absence of transportation costs.

- How confidentiality is maintained and personal information is protected. Clear explanation should be provided regarding the use and limits of technology with respect to secure (encrypted) and unsecure (unencrypted) communications, such as text/mobile messaging. Guidance is provided on which type of technology should be used for secure communications and which may be used for administrative tasks such as scheduling.
- The Coaching Agreement will also reference the aforementioned Privacy Policy, outlining the standards and procedures that will be adhered to regarding data protection, storage, management and transmission of protected health information. A statement identifying the coach as the owner of the coaching record including all transcripts, notes and emails (unless otherwise specified through law in the coach's geographic location or code of ethics) will also be provided. The client is informed that posting direct information about the coach or verbatim information from sessions is prohibited.
- Differentiate between online coaching services, tele-mental health services, crisis intervention services, etc.
- The client is informed about how to proceed if a technology breakdown occurs during a session, for example, 'If we disconnect, try to reconnect within ten minutes. If reconnection is not possible, email or call to reschedule an appointment'.
- Coaches are aware of their ethical responsibilities and have a clear understanding of online crisis intervention (suicidal/homicidal emails, texts or voice mails in the middle of the night, threatening posts on social media/forums, etc.), and research local resources within the client's geographic area as emergency backup resources.
- How cultural specifics may impact treatment. Coaches discuss varying time zones, cultural differences and language barriers that may impact the delivery of services. Coaches should also ensure that at, or prior to, the start of coaching, the client's expectations of the service being offered (such as the meaning of the term 'coaching') is sufficiently close to their own understanding and should consider that different cultures around the world can have different understandings of these matters.
- Coaches discuss with clients the expected boundaries and expectations about forming relationships online. Coaches inform clients that any requests for 'friendship', business contacts, direct or @replies, blog responses or requests for a blog response within social media sites will be ignored to preserve the integrity of the coaching relationship and protect confidentiality. If the client has not been formally informed of these boundaries prior to the coach receiving the request, the coach will ignore the request and explain why in subsequent interaction with the client.
- Coaches will seek to avoid conflicts of interest, and potential conflicts of interest, and if a conflict arises openly, disclose this and offer to remove themselves, providing a referral when such a conflict arises.

Coaches conduct an initial interview and evaluate the client's ability to effectively engage in technology-enabled coaching

The initial interview and intake process begins with the potential client's first contact. The coach implements informal measures for screening a client's suitability for the delivery of coaching services via technology:

- Client's Technology Skills: Coaches screen potential clients' use of technology through questions at the outset. Questions include, but are not limited to, an inquiry about the client's experience with online culture (e.g. email, chat rooms, forums, social networks, instant messaging, online purchasing, mobile texting, VOIP or telephones). Coaches ensure that the client's platform is compatible with the varying programmes and platforms that the coach may utilise during the course of coaching.
- Client's Language Skills: Coaches screen for language skills from the initial contact through the first few exchanges. Assessing for language barriers, reading and comprehension skills as well as cultural differences is part of the screening process. Text-based coaching may also involve screening for keyboarding proficiency.
- Client's Potential to Benefit from Coaching: Coach refers clients presenting with acute emotional distress or other symptoms of significant mental distress or disorder to appropriate mental health services.

Coaches seek out training, knowledge and mentoring and/ or supervision

Training, knowledge and mentoring regarding coaching and technology are paramount to delivering services that are considered 'best practice'. Coaches are encouraged to demonstrate proficiency and competency through formal training for online work; consulting books, peer-reviewed literature and popular media. Coach and/or peer mentoring and support are highly recommended for all coaches. Coaches keep themselves informed of new technologies, practices, legal requirements and standards relevant to the coaching profession. Examples of topics of study related to training, knowledge and supervision include but are not limited to:

- Online coaching
- Online crisis intervention best practice
- Online coaching supervision and online peer supervision
- Ethics of online coaching
- Avatar coaching
- Cybercoaching
- Text-based coaching

- Telehealth and distinctions
- Tele-mental health and distinctions
- Social media opportunity and limitations
- Mixed reality
- Online relationship dynamics
- Online peer support
- SMS text messaging
- Virtual worlds (i.e. Second Life) and virtual reality
- Coaching and technology
- Formal Training: Coaches seek out sufficient formal training whenever possible through college, university, accredited coaching institutes or private settings; and any such training is accurately displayed on the coach's website.
- Informal Training: Coaches complete CE and professional development and attend conferences, conventions and workshops.
- Books: Coaches read professional books written by the general public and professionals credentialed in their field.
- Peer-reviewed Literature: Coaches read peer-reviewed literature that includes the latest theories and research.
- Popular Media: Coaches are informed through popular media such as magazines, newspapers, social networking sites, websites, television and films, and understand the impact of coaching and technology on popular culture.
- Coach/Peer Mentoring: Mentoring is often sought by coaches who deliver services via technology, and can be delivered either face to face, over the phone or via encrypted methods.

Issues with social media

The Ethical Framework for Technology-delivered Coaching described in the previous chapter delineated specific ethical guidelines regarding the coach's use of social media for engagement. While these ethical guidelines are not nearly as stringent as they are for mental health practitioners (Kolmes *et al.*, 2011), coaches should still be diligent regarding proper engagement with clients on social media platforms. The following ethical dilemmas (Anthony and Nagel, 2009) are offered to begin to conceptualise the relationship with social media and how to preserve the integrity of the coaching relationship.

LinkedIn

Issues of power differential abound in this scenario

You have been seeing Jane in your face-to-face practice for six months. She is an active part of the community – town council, board member of two local non-profits, and she owns a gift shop on Main Street. In fact, you were recently asked to become a board member of the non-profit in which she sits as Chair. Jane has recently added you as a contact on LinkedIn. As both of you have a prominence in the community, she thought it would be good to link up. After all, both of you have contacts in common and she expects you will be working closely together on the same board giving your time to a worthy cause.

Not only would the coach and client be on the same board, but the client would also be in a position of authority over the coach. This creates a power differential in the two types of relationship that could impact on the valuable aims of the coaching itself.

The second issue involves social media. By being mutual contacts on LinkedIn, there is a possibility for confidentiality to be breached as people may determine that the coach is in fact the client's coach. This could also be considered a dual relationship particularly if either party asks for a recommendation and/or endorsement.

Twitter

Bartering and breach of confidentiality issues are apparent in this scenario

John is a client of yours and you see him in your face-to-face practice. He also engages in coaching chat with you as he is comfortable with technology and cyberspace. In fact, he specialises in search engine optimisation. He has offered to improve your Google ranking and offered web marketing strategies to you during a previous therapy session. He comes across your Twitter profile and follows you. When you discover this, you note he has retweeted your tweets several times that day. He even sent a tweet with a link to your website stating what a great coach you are.

Different codes of ethics have varying wording regarding bartering. Bartering is acceptable in some cultures and disciplines, but bartering is usually arranged due to financial constraints of the client. The item or service bartered must match the value of the coaching so as not to abuse power within the coaching relationship.

The second issue here is social media-microblogging. A blog is a public social media site, and the coach may have a difficult time monitoring all followers. Anyone can 'follow' a person's tweets without actually following. The issue here is the client's attempts to communicate with the coach via a social media site and promoting the coach's services – both could breach confidentiality. The coach should discuss these implications with the client. If social media is included in the coach's informed consent already, this is a time to revisit that agreement.

Directory listing

Concerns of policy in the event of non-contracted coaching emails are evident in this scenario

You typically start your day with a cup of coffee, your laptop and the chance to catch up on emails. It is 7:00 A.M. and you receive an email from highstakes123@ yahoo.com, generated from your listing in the Online Coach Directory. The email states the following,

I am so desperate. I lost my job yesterday and I have not told my wife. I do not know what to do – I owe huge $$ to this loan shark – I gambled my way into a mess. I just don't know- I mean I think my family would be better off if I just off myself. Can you help?

You note the email was sent at 2:00 A.M. Another email was sent directly to you from the same address at 3:00 A.M.

I sent you an email from some listing I found of you – did you get it?? Can you help??

What is your obligation to this person? In this case, you should email back, remove the content he sent and let him know his email was received and refer him to an appropriate crisis hotline or other online resource more appropriate for therapeutic intervention. Let him know that you are concerned and will make every effort to be sure he is safe. Give him a short timeframe to make contact. If no contact, call the authorities and ask how to proceed. Document your efforts.

Testimonial website

Issues of endorsement and confidentiality are evident in this scenario

Your colleague has created a listing on a website that offers people the opportunity to give feedback about services. This site offers information, critique and feedback on various service-oriented professionals, from chiropractors and massage therapists to consultants and coaches. Your colleague has positive feedback. Several clients have stated how much they benefited from their coaching experience with your colleague. A couple of people have given your colleague poor feedback. Your colleague responds to everyone who gives feedback including negative feedback.

More and more directories and websites are offering the ability for consumers to give feedback on a variety of professional services. Coaches should be careful not to solicit direct feedback from clients. For some disciplines, this is considered unethical (asking for an endorsement). Additionally, a client may be able to post feedback and a rating but may choose not to blind his or her identity. So, anyone reading the feedback can see who gave it and even access an email address in some cases. In this scenario, the coach actually comments back to the clients, praising those that give positive feedback and offering to renegotiate the coaching or defend actions to those who gave negative feedback, bringing the coaching relationship to the open web.

Facebook

Issues of professional identity and boundaries are evident this scenario

You attend the annual conference for your professional association and meet up with colleagues you have not seen in a while. Your quiet night out with a few friends turns into dinner, drinks, conversation and reminiscing. You had such a great time! When you return home and check email, you find several posts are waiting for you on your Facebook wall. You login to Facebook and see that you and your colleagues are tagged in several 'questionable' photos. The pictures reveal your fun night out and not necessarily from the most professional angle.

It is not always easy to keep a completely professional profile online. In this case, even with all of the privacy filters in place, and while you can remove the 'tag' feature on the picture, the picture remains in your colleague's online Facebook photo album for mutual friends and colleagues to see.

In summary, coaches are advised to utilise social media to advertise their coaching business and to educate the general public. Engaging with clients via the Internet and social media applications is not advised.

Privacy laws

In the United Kingdom and Europe, the General Data Protection Regulation (GDPR) concerning the Internet and confidentiality impacts almost all work online; and there are two versions of GDPR to be aware of since the United Kingdom left Europe. In the United States, the Health Insurance Portability and Accountability Act (HIPAA) is the regulatory law that speaks to confidentiality of patient records. There are similarities and differences between the two (Tovino, 2016). The following are brief statements about how each impacts those who practice online.

GDPR (both the United Kingdom and European Union) was enacted to confirm that laws governing personal data protection were updated, and businesses were careful with the handling of individuals' data. It is less prescriptive than the Data Protection Act of 1998 and considers the needs of the professional in transferring data as part of their work as legitimate need.

HIPAA is primarily concerned with third-party insurance payors and protecting Patient Health Information (PHI). While the Ethical Framework for Technology-delivered Coaching speaks to the use of encryption for online communication with clients, it may be assumed that coaches do not need to be HIPAA compliant. The exception to this may be for health and wellness coaches working within Employee Assistance Programs (EAP) or medical settings. If the coach is working under the umbrella of an organisation that is obligated to HIPAA regulations, the chances are that the coach will be held to that standard as well.

It should be noted that coaches who practice across international borders may need to be responsible to more than one privacy law.

Conclusion

This Ethical Framework for the use of Technology in Coaching was created, and is regularly revised, with the working coach in mind. We offer all our Ethical Frameworks free to the profession at the Online Therapy Institute website and are indebted to Ellen Neilly-Ritter of the Institute for Life Coach Training (ILCT) for her collaboration.

The future of ethics in the coaching profession with relevance to the field of technological use remains mysterious – at least until the next wave of new technologies arrive. Consider the potential for holographic coaches, where the blend of technology and live feed can mean a face-to-face 3D projection of both coach and coachee communicating in the same non-virtual space, taking us full circle back to face-to-face coaching contracts conducted imperceptibly at a distance.

Much of the ethical work done by the authors and their associates stems from the world of therapy, allowing an easy transition to the work done by coaches. By including some of this work in therapy field within this chapter, we hope to help clarify the ethical and legal position of those professionals who straddle the two professions.

References

Anthony, K. and Nagel, D.M. (2009). 'First International E-Mental Health Summit 2009, Amsterdam Poster Session', *Ethical Implications for Therapists Who Work and Socialize in Cyberspace*.

Anthony, K. and Nagel, D.M. (2010). *Online Therapy: A Practical Guide*. London: Sage.

Anthony, K. and Nagel, D. (2012). *A Brave New World: Coaching Online,* Issue 1. Coaching Today. Lutterworth: BACP Publications, pp. 33–37.

Anthony, K., Nagel, D.M. and Goss, S. (2020). 'The Ethical Framework for Technology-delivered Coaching: A Summary', in *Coaching Today*, vol. 36. Lutterworth: BACP Publications, pp. 20–21.

Feltham, C. and Hanley, T. (2017). 'What Are Counselling and Psychotherapy?', in C. Feltham, T. Hanley and L.A. Winter (eds.), *The Sage Handbook of Counselling and Psychotherapy*. London: Sage.

Goss, S. (2011). 'Research Review: Online Coaching Research, the Future Is Bright!', *Therapeutic Innovations in Light of Technology*, 1(4), pp. 14–17.

Kanatouri, S. (2020). *The Digital Coach*. London: Routledge.

Kolmes, K., Nagel, D.M. and Anthony, K. (2011). 'An Ethical Framework for the Use of Social Media by Mental Health Professionals', *Therapeutic Innovations in Light of Technology*, 1(3), pp. 20–29.

Labardee, L., Nagel, D.M. and Anthony, K. (2011). 'An Ethical Framework for the Use of Technology in Coaching', *Therapeutic Innovations in Light of Technology*, 1(4), pp. 20–28.

Nagel, D.M. (2016). 'In the News: What Is the Difference Between a Coach and a Therapist?', *Employee Assistance Report*, 4(19), p. 7.

Nagel, D.M. and Anthony, K. (2011). 'Coaching & Counselling – Is There a Merge of Disciplines on the Horizon?', *Therapeutic Innovations in Light of Technology*, 2(1), pp. 24–29.

Nagel, D.M., Ritter, E.N. and Anthony, K. (2019). 'The Institute for Life Coach Training', *Ethical Framework for Technology-delivered Coaching*. www.lifecoachtraining.com/techcoaching [accessed 12 December 2020].

Tovino, S.A. (2016). 'The HIPAA Privacy Rule and the EU GDPR: Illustrative Comparisons', *Seton Hall Law Review*, 47, p. 973.

Chapter 7

Essential psychosocial aspects of cyberculture

In the off-line world, we are trained from birth to initiate or respond to human beings presented to us with the intention of communicating. It is natural to be in conversation with someone, whether personal or professional, in a physical environment. This natural state of being has been disrupted by technology in being able to communicate with other humans without a physical environment being mutually shared. Our experience of this before the Internet meant that we passively watched rather than actively doing, as evidenced by TV and theatrical productions. We may react to the screen but feel no compulsion or expectation to respond to it.

This life training in the Western world results in the need for a close examination of what is happening psychologically for participants of online coaching, as it takes place. In the authors' opinion, the three essential psychological processes to know about and consider are Perceived anonymity, Disinhibition, Presence and fantasy (small f).

Perceived anonymity

Research (Zajonc, 1965) suggests that people engage and perform better when alone rather than in the presence of one or two people. Zajonc's study revealed that a person's response to being in the presence of another is that of tension and alertness, and with a feeling of being judged. The concept of social anonymity explains why some clients reach out for online coaching via email, chat and voice. Social anonymity can prove positive when the client and the coach are aware that the anonymity is purposefully sought by the client. The client may perceive the coaching session as a safe environment with this anonymity built in. One study (Lombardi and Ciceri, 2016) suggests that privacy is a supportive condition for some psychological processes involved in human well-being, such as increasing the sense of control over the environment. This study supports the idea that a client may experience the coaching session more positively with anonymity.

DOI: 10.4324/9781315685939-8

The online disinhibition effect

Online disinhibition describes our tendency to lose social inhibitions when not in the physical presence of another person. First described by Suler in 2001 and revised in 2004, it is widely recognised as an essential psychological consideration when working with our coachees.

Reading of Suler's original paper is encouraged, but we can summarise the disinhibition effect using his headings (Anthony and Nagel, 2013):

You don't know me (dissociative anonymity)

The Internet offers apparent anonymity – if you wish, you can keep your identity hidden and use any name, either close to your own (e.g. KatAnt) or far away (e.g. Xyz123). For the most part, people only know what you choose to tell them about yourself. When people have the opportunity to separate their actions from their real world and identity, they feel less vulnerable about opening up. They also feel less need to be accountable for their actions – in fact, people may even convince themselves that those behaviours 'aren't me at all'. In psychology, this is called 'dissociation'.

You can't see me (invisibility)

In many online environments, other people cannot see you. As you browse through websites, message boards and even some chat rooms, people may not even know you are there at all. In text communication such as email, chat, blogs and instant messaging others may know a great deal about who you are. However, they still cannot see or hear you – and you cannot see or hear them. Even with everyone's identity visible, the opportunity to be physically invisible amplifies the disinhibition effect. Invisibility gives people the courage to go to places and do things that they otherwise would not, often with undesirable results.

See you later (asynchronicity)

In email and message boards, communication is asynchronous. People do not interact with each other in real time. Some may take minutes, hours, days or even months to reply to something you say. Not having to deal with someone's immediate reaction can be disinhibiting. In email and message boards, where there are delays in feedback, people's train of thought may progress more steadily and quickly towards deeper expressions of what they are thinking and feeling in comparison to instantaneous communications. Some people may even experience asynchronous communication as 'running away' after posting a message that is personal, emotional or hostile. It feels safe putting it 'out there', where it can be left behind.

It's all in my head (solipsistic introjection or egoistic self-absorption)

The absence of the visual and aural cues of face-to-face communication combined with text communication can have other interesting effects on people. Reading another person's message may be experienced as a voice within one's head, as if that person has been magically inserted or 'introjected' into one's psyche, similar to how we hear a character when reading a book. In fact, consciously or unconsciously, we may even assign a visual image to what we think that person looks like and how that person behaves. The online companion now becomes a character within personal mental experience of the world. Online text communication can become the psychological tapestry in which a person's mind weaves fantasy role-plays, usually unconsciously and with considerable disinhibition.

It's just a game (dissociative imagination)

If we combine the feeling that all these conversations are going on inside our own heads with the nature of cyberspace as a means to escape real life, we get a slightly different force that magnifies disinhibition. People may feel that the imaginary characters they 'created' exist in a way that is quite separate from everyday life – a different realm altogether. It is possible to split or 'dissociate' online fiction from offline fact. Once they turn off the computer and return to their daily routine, they believe they can leave that game and their game-identity behind. Why should they be held responsible for what happens in that make-believe play world that has nothing to do with offline reality?

We're equals (minimising authority)

While online, others may not know a person's status in the offline world, and it may not have as much impact as it does in that world. In most cases, everyone on the Internet has an equal opportunity to voice him or herself. Although one's status in the outside world ultimately may have some impact on one's powers in cyberspace, what mostly determines your influence on others is your skill in communicating. People are reluctant to say what they really think as they stand before an authority figure, but online, in what feels like a peer relationship – with the appearances of 'authority' minimised – it is much easier to speak out and think, 'Well, what can they do to me?'

While we posit that disinhibition is a vital consideration within online coaching, research has not yet shown it is universal. Recognition and mutual consideration of the possibility of disinhibition for both coach and coachee (professionals are just as subject to the effect as non – professionals) is required. Future research as to the evidence of the Online Disinhibition Effect is much needed.

Creating and maintaining telepresence

Consider the statement at the start of this chapter:

We may react to the screen but feel no compulsion or expectation to respond to it.

This learned passivity is utterly useless in the online coaching environment. Passivity may include involuntary reactions, such as nodding on the telephone. In Distance Coaching, you will not share the same physical environment as your coachee, where your coaching skills may feel more natural and voluntary because it is backed up by your physical presence – the intricacies and nuances of body language; and timing of non-vocal minimal encouragers such as 'mm-hmm' or 'uh-huh'.

The word we used to describe professional coaching skills when online is *intentional*. This applies to the online coach and their environment. There is a need to be explicitly present within your own (coaching) environment for you to feel present to your client at the other end of the connection. According to Lombard and Ditton (1997) with reference to non-communicative technologies, the concept of presence can be:

- **Presence as social richness** – the extent to which a medium is perceived as *sociable, warm, sensitive, personal or intimate* when it is used to interact with other people.
- **Presence as realism** – the degree to which a medium can produce *seemingly accurate representations of objects, events and people* – representations that look, sound and/or feel like the 'real thing'.
- **Presence as transportation** – '*You are there*', in which the user is transported to another place; '*It is here*', in which another place and the objects within it are transported to the user; and '*We are together*' in which two (or more) communicators are transported together to a place that they share.
- **Presence as immersion** – including a psychological component. When users feel immersive presence, they are *involved, absorbed, engaged* and *engrossed.*
- **Presence as social actor within medium** – users' perceptions and the resulting psychological processes lead them to *illogically overlook the mediated* or even artificial nature of an entity within a medium and attempt to interact with it.

In our experience, the most applicable definition in the online coaching environment is Presence as Transportation, although always with an eye on Presence as social actor as the goal *if we are trying to replicate an off-line session experience in terms of presence as we may recognise it from traditional coaching training.* Each of the definitions usually has a part to play, and usually to a greater or lesser extent. Recognising where you sit on the telepresence spectrum allows you to adjust or improve techniques to achieve greater telepresence.

Transportation into cyberspace should include intentionally clearing your psychological space as you prepare to enter the session to join your client. Pre-session preparation becomes important in online work, as does transition out of the session at the end. This can be compared to driving to and from a coaching session in the off-line world – not only a function that has to happen to enable the work but also one that can become part of the work. For the professional coach, preparation of your space to conduct the session is often part of the psychological clearance – sometimes intentionally ritualistic to bring the mind and body in line with the intention of the forthcoming work being successful and useful.

Just as we should be prepared for discussion with the client about the possibility of experiencing the Online Disinhibition Effect, we may also share the usefulness (or not) of the client creating their own preparation strategies for both beginning and ending the session. This can be as simple as a bath, or solo cup of tea in a favourite chair – the point is to enter the right frame of mind to do the work in the midst of demands on our time from everyday life.

An online coaching service at this point in time is still reaching for the familiarity of an off-line coaching relationship in line with core training. It is most likely that the coaches of the future, who do not remember life without technology and the Internet, will fully embrace the online relationship as the norm – as is likely to be the case for society as a whole. This simple premise remains currently abhorrent, yet the 2020 pandemic has already somewhat normalised this anthropological change.

Working with fantasy (small f)

One definition of the word 'fantasy' is that it is *the power or process of creating especially unrealistic or improbable mental images in response to psychological need <an object of fantasy>; also: a mental image or a series of mental images so created* (adapted from www.merriam-webster.com/dictionary/fantasy).

We use the term fantasy in this book to show what the creative human mind can produce to 'fill in gaps' in light of a lack of knowledge of a physical presence, and without aural or visual cues.

The fantasy of the other person or persons in a coaching setting is an interesting facet of the relationship dynamic. Many practitioners have photos and descriptions of their personal circumstances posted on their websites, but these static images and words can never fulfil what the client wants to believe about the person with whom they are in online communication. Even with a video introduction, the client will fill in gaps!

Without a physical presence or voice, the client often forms an idealised picture of the person who is sharing their journey – there are many gaps that they want to fill, and the picture they develop over the course of the relationship can vary in accuracy. With no physical clues given on a website, even the gender of the change agent can be mistaken if the name is ambiguous (Kim, Sam, Chris, etc.), and initial emails can set up an erroneous fantasy that has the potential to be shattered when the truth emerges, often as the practitioner has assumed the client 'knows' about him or her. The relationship is often irreparably damaged.

As an example, in a therapeutic setting, consider the experience of journalist Sue Webster, who explored the concept of receiving online therapy and opened a therapeutic relationship with Kim Smith of www.onlinecounselling.co.uk. She had a fantasy that she was talking (writing) to a woman, saying:

> *If it's hard to describe what took place in those sessions, that is only because the intangibles in any therapeutic relationship are its main point. But I felt accepted and understood, no matter how shocking or shameful the situations I posed might be. Of course, I didn't see or hear Kim, but I responded to her challenges and felt her empathy. If I shilly-shallied with excuses, she saw through them; if I was self-pitying, she was ironic; but if I was honest and thoughtful, she seemed to embrace me through her words.*
>
> *She was the wise, generous mother I had always wished for.*
>
> *Although I knew on one level that this idealisation was a fantasy, I still felt let down when I eventually made telephone contact with her. In fact, I was absolutely furious. Kim Smith is a man. A very nice, sympathetic man with a northern accent who used to live on a boat and admits to wearing sandals with socks. He wasn't what I had in mind – but once I had adjusted to the new reality, I had to admit that this was surely a positive aspect to online counselling.*

Clients also have a fantasy about how their counsellor sounds, reportedly sometimes giving them a voice that is calm, slow and gentle because that is how they read the emails or text chat as it appears on the screen in front of them.

Of course, any seriously erroneous fantasies should be set straight as soon as possible – any online relationship has the potential for a misunderstanding about the relationship's nature, and erotic transference or projection is easily facilitated in such an intimate space.

Understanding transference/countertransference within the coaching process is important. This phenomenon occurs within in-person coaching sessions and, paired with the Online Disinhibition Effect, the authors posit that transference/countertransference is heightened online.

Transference and countertransference are psychological processes first conceptualised by Freud (Freud and Breuer, 2004) in his 1895 book, *Studies in Hysteria*. In the context of therapy, transference refers to redirection of a client's feelings for a significant person to the therapist. Countertransference is defined as redirection of a therapist's feelings towards a client, and the emotional entanglement that may ensue.

Berglas (2002) suggests that understanding transference and countertransference is as important for coaches as for mental health professionals. He suggests that without a rudimentary understanding of these processes, a coach may overlook the need for a referral to counselling or therapy for some coach clients.

De Haan (2011) suggests that coaches first realise their own countertransference. Within the coaching relationship, this begins with the coach feeling that the first tendency at the start of the relationship is to be sure that the client 'likes' the coach. This is particularly prominent with new coaches just starting out and is a normal response, but one that can be altered once the coach is aware. Once this is addressed, the coach can attend to the client's transference from the start. The coach can pick up on cues, defences and anxieties, and guide the client in determining their authentic wishes behind them. If, in this process, the defences and anxieties appear to be more than situational and are blocking the client from goal attainment, a proper referral to a mental health professional is in order.

Of course, the coaching relationship should never become personal over professional, and in most cases this element of working online never arises. Our point is that the online coach has an awareness of psychological elements that occur uniquely online in comparison to off-line work and uses that awareness intentionally within the work not least to avoid ruptures to the online coaching relationship.

Conclusion

These psychosocial elements of working online are fairly generalisable but we must not lose sense of the individual. Furthermore, it is these areas we feel warrant more research – in particular around the mostly anecdotal evidence we have of Disinhibition Effect.

References

Anthony, K. and Nagel, D. (2013). 'Appreciating Cyberculture and the Virtual Self Within', *Self & Society*, 40(3), pp. 25–28.

Berglas, S. (2002). 'The Very Real Dangers of Executive Coaching', *Harvard Business Review*, 80(6), pp. 86–92, 153.

De Haan, E. (2011). 'Back to Basics: How the Discovery of Transference Is Relevant for Coaches and Consultants Today', *International Coaching Psychology Review*, 6, pp. 180–193.

Feltham, C. and Hanley, T. (2017). *Sage Handbook of Counselling and Psychotherapy*. London: Sage.

Freud, S. and Breuer, J. (2004). *Studies in Hysteria*. New York: Penguin Books, p. xxi.

Lombard, M. and Ditton, T. (1997). 'At the Heart of It All: the Concept of Presence', *Journal of Computer – Mediated Communication*, 2(3).

Lombardi, D.B. and Ciceri, M.R. (2016). 'More Than Defense in Daily Experience of Privacy: The Functions of Privacy in Digital and Physical Environments', *Europe's Journal of Psychology*, 12(1), pp. 115–136. www.ncbi.nlm.nih.gov/pmc/articles/PMC4873070/

Nagel, D.M. (2016). 'In the News: What Is the Difference between a Coach and a Therapist?', *Employee Assistance Report*, 19(8), p. 7.

Nagel, D.M. and Anthony, K. (2011). 'Coaching & Counselling – Is There a Merge of Disciplines on the Horizon?', *Therapeutic Innovations in Light of Technology*, 2(1), pp. 24–29.

Suler, J. (2004). 'The Online Disinhibition Effect', *Cyberpsychology & Behavior*, 7(3), pp. 321–326.

Zajonc, R.B. (1965). 'Social Facilitation', *Science*, 149(3681), pp. 269–274.

Chapter 8

Creating a continual professional development programme as an online coach

Introduction

As an established coach, it seems reasonable to assume that you have had a core training. In addition, it is likely that you attend workshops, conferences and various other occasions that are educational in nature and which give you a wider view of not just your own coaching practice but also that of your colleagues in the field. It may also be the case that you attend occasions that encompass the work of those in what could be considered sister professions, such as the fields of therapy and counselling, or complementary and alternative medicine (CAMS) such as using essential oils as a strategy for maintaining overall well-being.

In addition to pursuing events for your own interest and simply to inform your work, it may be the case that your professional organisation states a requirement for a certain number of hours annually. This is to ensure your practice is up to date and relevant, although the actual activity you undertake is usually self-nominated (albeit sometimes under a defined heading such as a certain number of hours under the heading of 'ethics'). This is generally referred to as Continuing Professional Development (CPD) or Continuing Education (CE). The point of such activity is to ensure that your practice remains relevant to the field, to evidence that you are a committed coach with a responsibility for your own ongoing learning, and to show that you are able to reflect on your own practice to enhance your work and therefore give a better service to your clients.

There is a difference between your professional organisation requiring evidence of CPD activity and your employer demanding it. The latter is generally paid for by the employer and can be considered training, whereas CPD is generally sought by you as an individual practitioner. As defined by Johnstone (2019), key features of CPD activity need to:

• Be a documented process
• Be self-directed, driven by you not your employer
• Focus on learning from experience, reflective learning and review
• Help you set development goals and objectives
• Include both formal and informal learning

DOI: 10.4324/9781315685939-9

workshop, need not be the only method of gathering knowledge and those vital CPD hours. While attending events that take place in a physical sense (being 'in-room') are just as relevant as ever, we can add online events to our CPD toolboxes in a formal sense and add online professional networking in a casual sense. The opportunities to gather ongoing learning about new techniques, tools, theories and practice have exploded in recent years, mainly because of improved broadband being available – almost as standard in most parts of the world. This means that live video and audio streaming gives us the benefit of attending CPD events without actually needing to be there.

If you are not familiar with attending CPD events remotely, or completing formal training online, it may seem a lonely activity. This can be the case when simply watching a presentation live or scrolling through an expert's slides after the event. However, most live events that take place online include a chat room where you can interact with other attendees and the presenter via text while the event is taking place, which makes for a dynamic way of gaining CPD hours without the additional expense and time taken to travel to a different destination.

In this chapter, we shall examine some of the activities you should seek to undertake in order to be a current and relevant coach practicing in the modern digitally connected world. These can apply equally to those planning to or having a current practice online, or those with just an offline practice, although the examples we shall look at apply to being an online coaching practitioner.

Formal training programmes

The general consensus within the helping professions in the UK states that to train as an online practitioner, the selected training programme should be conducted online (Anthony, 2014), and this is borne out by the recommendations of various professional organisations such as the BACP, which includes a lively Coaching Division. This is because the purpose of the training is to learn how to transfer current coaching skills to the online environment, and not to learn how to be a coach itself (although such trainings are widely available). In order to learn how to transfer coaching communication skills to online communication platforms, it makes sense to train in that way and immerse yourself in the modality in which you will be working.

To illustrate our points here, we will use the Online Therapy Institute approach to training:

> In our view, there are two elements of training content that are essential in becoming a rounded online practitioner: a foundation in the concepts and practice of online behaviour itself, and on which we touched in Chapter 1 (Cyberculture); and the practical skills in using various technologies to conduct a coaching relationship between two or more human beings. Our own trainings are held entirely online via an online learning platform (currently Pathwright). In this way, we can offer our own reading material, show videos,

require live experiential exercises (such as participation in chat rooms or searching for online coaching websites) and link to further reading of relevant blogs, articles and academic papers. We offer a short course for coaches who have already completed core training as a life, business or health coach. The short course focuses specifically on online coaching. We also offer a comprehensive course covering life, wellness and psychospiritual coaching with the topic of technology-assisted coaching embedded within. The courses concentrate more on practical elements of the coaching relationship as it takes place via mainly email, chat rooms/instant messaging, telephone and audio routes, and video conferencing. Within the course other elements of communication conducted via technology are included, such as virtual reality environments and using brief text messaging between mobile/cell phones. Certain elements of coach practice which transfer well to the online environment, such as using vision boards, also have their place within the training.

Trainings online such as the one used as an example above can often be a silent way of training when it is just ourselves and our electronic device accessing the online programme! To combat this, we schedule live telephone or video catch-ups with the tutor or tutors involved, and also make ourselves available for one-to-one conversations when desired or needed by the trainee. We include as many different media as we can, such as documentary film preloaded into the course via YouTube embedding.

Undertaking lengthy training programmes as part of our continuing professional development can involve a financial outlay often beyond our means. It is wise to seek out programmes that can be taken in a modular fashion, or for which the cost can be spread via payment plans.

It is worth assessing the time you have to give to a formal CPD training course before applying, as well as considering financial commitments. As online courses can be delivered around the clock if they are asynchronous in nature, with the trainee deciding when during the day (or night) to access the course material, these may be better suited to a coach who has a busy practice to run as well as the usual family commitments, as opposed to a course which requires in-person attendance on a regular basis.

Be prepared, when booking online CPD and training that you are likely to encounter a wide range of fellow trainees from all over the world! This is particularly likely to be the case if the course or programme is delivered asynchronously, as participants do not have to attend live regular time slots. Taking part in such programmes can enhance and enrich your learning, as well as giving you more experience of different coaching cultures and how coaching technique is practiced internationally. Online courses generally have forums for student co-learning, and many have private Facebook groups for networking and sharing resources between trainees. Participation in the latter need not be compulsory as many practitioners remain uncomfortable with social networking in general. However, if you choose not to take part in every avenue of online communication and networking offered, you are likely to miss out on the full online learning experience.

Offline workshops and conferences

Authors' note: We draw your attention again to the foreword about this book being written during 2021 lockdown, with no knowledge about the availability of off-line workshops and conferences going forwards.

Offline workshops – that is, ones delivered in the traditional sense of in-room events – are also offered for the topic of online coaching. This may seem counter-intuitive, but in reality, they can be extremely useful for exploring possibilities of becoming an online practitioner without needing to sign up online for the numerous platforms involved in the delivery of online training and CPD events.

Becoming a member of an online networking coaching group, such as on LinkedIn, is a good way of finding out more about workshops delivered in your area and further afield. Many continue to be announced in traditional print media, such as coaching journals and magazines. It is worth noting here that increasingly workshops delivered in-room are being simultaneously broadcast live online, creating a hybrid workshop. For the offline attendee, it can be useful to revisit the recording after the event to refresh yourself with the information given, and also to catch any resources offered on the day – which are increasingly being delivered via email or as a download from a website after the event.

In the opinion of the authors, offline workshops and lectures on online coaching can really only deliver a snapshot of what it is like to actually practice online. That said, they can be an extremely valuable and cost-effective way of discovering the basics of online practice, and – more particularly – whether any of the ways of delivering coaching sessions electronically could be a good fit for you as a coach. For example, an offline workshop outlining the methods of potential online delivery such as email, chat rooms, videoconferencing and virtual environments could determine if you would be naturally affiliated to the more visual environments such as virtual worlds, but less comfortable in text-based environments such as email or chat rooms. Therefore, when designing your ongoing coaching CPD programme, you could seek online trainings and CPD that focus on your strengths as an offline coach rather than attempting to shoehorn yourself into a method of delivery that simply does not fit. Time and money spent on an offline exploratory workshop is usually a good way of avoiding time and money spent on online trainings that fail to enhance your overall coaching practice.

In the same way that offline workshops can be invaluable, offline conferences are also worth considering. If your professional organisation hosts an annual (or more frequent) conference, it is likely to have simultaneous strands of topics designed to grab your attention. If you are considering developing and expanding your coaching practice into the online environment, seek out strands that focus on online methods of delivery in particular. This may seem an obvious statement, but resistance to technology can often lead us to dismiss these valuable sessions if there are alternatives better placed within your comfort zone – and conferences that focus purely on online work are rare. You may wish to approach your professional organisation to suggest recognition of online work, or at least bring to their attention that there is a way of practicing coaching that needs more investigation and exploration – and that conferences and workshops are the easiest way to do this.

Online webinars and conferences

(Adapted from Wilson and Anthony, 2015, reproduced with permission).

For those of us who have spent time and money training and developing ourselves to help create and maintain whole human relationships, the idea of continuing our professional development on our own using an electronic device seems a long way from the heart of our profession's core intentions. In this section, we will consider the hows and whys of these learning experiences.

When in private practice, the time spent on travel is unpaid and someone has to foot that bill. In the 21st century, travel is expensive at any time of the year and included in the cost of any professional development is the cost of getting there, perhaps accommodation, and of course the need to return home. In addition, we live in times where we are much more aware of our carbon footprint – we are conscious that every mile spent travelling in a fossil-fuelled vehicle has an impact on our environment, which is rarely covered by the money that we pay for the privilege. Diluting our impact on the environment by reducing the miles we travel every year appeals to our environmentally responsible consciousness.

So, from a practical point of view, the journey to a learning experience being the walk across the kitchen floor, or the wander down the hall into the office, saves countless hours of travel, eliminates the stress of moving around the globe and significantly reduces our carbon footprint. The financial cost needs to be measured only in what we spend on Internet connection and devices.

As coaches, we are looking for a specific kind of learning experience. We are not accountants or bankers turning up at a conference for the latest legislation or the most up-to-date tools to increase profit margins. We are practitioners who embarked on a vocation with a desire to connect and be part of a profession which makes a difference to the lives of other human beings. When we come together to learn, we are also looking for that sense of connection for ourselves.

We recognise that there is a place for cutting-edge research, we want to know what our colleagues are developing in other parts of the field and we want to take home new ideas for our own practice and meet the amazing people with whom we have the privilege of working. But in addition, we need something for ourselves, to be nourished in our own work – we need food for our souls. Is it really possible to get that sitting on our own, in our own environment, in front of our electronic devices?

Companies turn up at an offline conference with cameras and computers and the filming is then viewable on their website. So, as you sit at your device you can see the speaker present, you can see their PowerPoint, and while there might be a ten-second delay between the speaker talking and you hearing through your computer, you are pretty much keeping up with the event as it happens.

But does it feel like you are actually there? You can hear it, and you can see it, but can you *feel* it? One of the most important aspects for coaches when we come together is that we are actually together. All those hours in practice rooms with clients can feel isolating from other practitioners, especially in private practice when most of the people we would see in a working week are coming to us for assistance. So, we need that time together to be nourished by each other. Is that really replicable online?

To answer this question, we are passionate about the presence of a chat room at Online Therapy Institute events. Having a passive television experience works fine when watching our favourite soaps or an exciting movie, but it will not give us the sense of connection that we need from learning experiences. The chat room is central to the experience of being at an event online and allows participants to see each other in a different way than is possible at a venue. The chat room is a box on the web page next to the video window with a space to enter thoughts in the form of text, and as each participant does this, there is an ongoing roll of text which looks similar to a play script. Each participant's name shows up in the left-hand side (usually) of the page, with whatever they have chosen to type next to it.

The experience this creates is reminiscent of what Suler describes in his work on the disinhibition effect (2004) and is an important element of cyberculture as discussed in Chapter 1. To recap, Suler proposes that when we communicate online, we lose some of the inhibitions that are present when we are physically in the room with someone, such as the impact of our consciousness of our own body shape or that of the other; the social conventions that we have absorbed throughout childhood and the fear of how the others in the interaction are perceiving us. Being online, where we are not able to see the bodies of those we are interacting with and they cannot see ours, we are protected from the experience of seeing the other person's reaction to us in their facial expressions and this allows us to be disinhibited in ways that we might find surprising.

This has been the role of the chat room at our online events. At many conference occasions, you may have sat at a conference and had a question for the presenter that you would love to ask, but to speak in front of a room of peers has felt overwhelming. Or you may have wanted to question a leader in the field, to offer him or her another perspective, but felt daunted in doing so. When it comes from a deeply passionate and experienced place within us, such interaction may feel like a cardinal sin in contradicting someone we might perceive to hold so much power.

The disinhibition effect changes those dynamics – suddenly the speaker is confronted with an audience they cannot see, and if you make a comment or ask a question, no one can see you. You can type the question, maybe retype it, and even if it comes out wrong, no one can see you blushing! The narrowing of the gap between those who have been able to write and research and publish and present, and those in the profession who feel small and without much to contribute, is something the chat room offers.

The hushed silence of the conference centre while a presentation is taking place is not reflected in the chat room, as the presenter delivers we are all having continual reactions, thoughts, ideas and inspirations which do not need to be contained. These can be voiced in this text environment without an audible interruption to the speaker. For some of the more technologically advanced conferences, delegates in the conference centre are also able to contribute to the chat room during the presentation. The cross fertilisation of ideas from practitioners located in the venue with those located in their homes or offices – or even on the train – around the globe is extremely exciting.

When presenters are also able to view and absorb the interaction from the chat room into their presentations, there is a learning experience co-created by all who are present both in body and virtually. This represents an unprecedented learning opportunity for coaches to come together and inspire each other, whether we are privileged to deliver our ideas as presenters; can physically and financially afford to be in the venue; are at home in front of our laptops; or are on the train with our smartphones.

But that is about the learning, we are still not talking about the nourishing. For many people, the need for contact at professional development events can sometimes be the hardest part of conferencing. We may see someone across the room, or even sitting next to us, that looks as if they would be a good connection – perhaps they made a comment at a presentation earlier, or we can see by their name badge that they represent an organisation or work in a part of the field that we would love to know more about – but making that first audible sound by way of introduction can feel terrifying.

The feedback that we have had from events is that not being seen physically in the chat room has freed participants to be much more themselves. This means being able to be more sociable, and to interact with other delegates in ways that they have never been able to in the years of professional development events they have attended in-room. Never having felt able to offer a question or a comment to a presenter, they find themselves able to fully contribute to the debate and the discussion, including feeling valued as part of a group of passionate, inspired professionals who are able to come together in diversity and openness to hear and learn from each other. And of course, to be nourished in that contact!

In most of the Western world, coaching is still predominantly the preserve of the white middle classes, those of us who are privileged enough to have lifestyles that produce enough time and resources to spend years training without the guarantee of income. But what does that mean for those of us that do not have those resources, who are not from the social and ethnic groups that dominate conference events in large venues that have been built and then hired at great expense? What about those of us who cannot access those events due to limited financial and physical resources?

The opportunity of not being excluded from these experiences is vital for opening access to all of us in the field whatever our resources and experience. Having the option of turning up in the chat room with only the name that we have chosen to show our fellow participants is an experience that can free us to be who we truly are as practitioners, and to offer ourselves to each other in a way that is less inhibited and therefore more nourishing.

However, online environments open up many more possibilities than just live-streaming offline conferences. For example, the Online Therapy Institute frequently delivers conferences in Second Life. To recap: Second Life is an online virtual environment that to the uninitiated looks something like a cartoon world. Each participant has an avatar that they use to move around in the virtual world and then interact with others. You may have heard of similar environments such as World of Warcraft, where participants come together to collaborate and compete to achieve a goal. Second Life is different in that it has no game scenario and there is no goal for the participants; it is simply a place to exist, and for that reason it lends itself well as an environment for collaboration, development and learning. The disinhibition effect is also experienced in Second Life; participants are able to shape and dress their avatars in ways that reflect themselves, their personalities and of course their mood at the conference.

At such events in online worlds, presenters can educate practitioners from all over the globe; many of them are educators themselves and have logged into the conference in between teaching classes or faculty meetings to bring attendees their research, to offer their unique perspective on the field and to bring new and inspiring ideas to the participants. This means that catching the expertise of the presenters with no travel time, no travel cost and of course no travel stress is possible. And to do this in a window of opportunity in the presenter's day without any need to cancel classes creates a unique opportunity to bring together an international pool of expertise using little resources.

Academic peer-reviewed resources

One huge bonus of the Internet is that it has made access to academic papers and journals much more accessible than they were previously. Unfortunately, accessing the paper or article you want can be a very hit-and-miss process, as some publishing houses retain a paywall (the system by which you pay for access) for their products, whereas others have opened up access to all comers.

A good way of knowing what has been published or made available otherwise is to set up a Google Scholar alert direct to your inbox (https://scholar.google.co.uk for the United Kingdom, with alternative similar URLs available in other countries, .com in the United States, for example). From Google Scholar, you can set up a personal library, check where your own work has been cited elsewhere, see more general journal metrics and personalise your settings as to how these results are displayed (with more detail being offered via premium membership). By using the Google system, you are likely to capture the most widespread information about articles, papers and books. It is not a perfect system however – if another person has the same name as you, you will sometimes also be alerted to writing that is irrelevant to your work and study. However, on the whole, it can be a valuable tool, particularly as it will also recommend publications in the same field as your own personalised searches on the homepage.

Access to articles from journals that are tied to specific publishers have their own policies for accessing academic work and are too numerous to mention. However, in general you can read the abstracts of papers for free, and then either subscribe to the journal for frequent access (either online or in print format) or pay for each article individually as a download. Be prepared for how much individual access can cost however – this can vary from a few pounds, dollars or Euros to a quite hefty charge!

You can usually sign up to a journal as an individual, or it may be worth checking to see if an organisational or university subscription is available. Sometimes, access to a journal comes with your membership of a coaching organisation or division, such as the European Mentoring and Coaching Council (EMCC) or the Coaching Division of the BACP. Many print-based journals offer at least one free downloadable article from their publication as a taster.

Authors of papers appreciate being asked about their work, and if you are finding it difficult to track down the full copy of a paper, or it is too old to be offered by any of the usual routes, a polite email to the authors is generally well-received. They may send you their original manuscript or scan via email or know where it is buried online!

Non-academic resources – blogs and microblogs

The word blog is a truncation of 'web-log' and refers to a self-authored, or increasingly multi-authored, piece of writing that is made accessible to all. Blogs vary in length and of course topic and can be an extremely useful avenue to information and opinion on anything you need to know about. They are easy to set up, edit, add pictures or other images, and have many variations (for example, a vlog is a video blog, and a podcast is an audio blog). According to hostingtribunal.com, in 2021 there are approximately 500 million blogs in existence, more than a third of all websites are blogs, and less than 10% generate any income.

As a coach, you undoubtedly have valuable thoughts and theories about coaching work from which others would benefit. Blogging your work is the easiest route to disseminating information and is also a valuable way of driving traffic to your website. For this reason alone, it is worth setting aside some time each week to devote to regular updates and new blogposts. You can also allow comments from readers, which can be moderated (i.e. your approval is needed for them to be published online), and this interactive way of publishing can be a valuable networking tool in itself.

Two words of caution are required before you start blogging! Firstly, your coaching work is subject to the rules of confidentiality you have with your client and from your professional organisation, and any blogging that concerns client work or cases needs careful editing to disguise the client concerned (not to mention seeking their permission to use their case). You may think that your client's information, such as profession or location (even if as generally put as 'medical' and 'north-east'), is something unlikely to be recognisable, but with a potentially global audience, it can be surprisingly easy for someone somewhere to join the dots and identify the client.

Secondly, while open comments can create a rich seam of opinion and information, you may also find that this opens the blog up to criticism of your work and you personally. Blogging is subject to the effects of disinhibition as discussed earlier, and many people totally lose their self-editing skills when posting comments online.

Microblogging is the posting of resources within a limited number of characters (currently 280), and the best-known platform for this is Twitter. On Twitter, you can follow other people's 'tweets' and they can follow you back. Although Twitter is often in the media as a place where extremely unpleasant abuse can take place, its professional use in coaching can be invaluable as both a networking tool and to keep abreast of what is happening in the coaching world.

Keeping up with such aspects of working online are increasingly essential parts of continuing professional development, as well as necessary ways of developing your market share potential as outlined in Chapter 5.

The following case illustration is from Darlene Ouimet, a certified international coach, inspirational speaker and author of the high-traffic emotional healing blog 'Emerging from Broken'. It is published with permission and shows us just how life-changing writing a regular blog can be! A longer version is available from the reference:

> When I overcame dissociative issues and chronic depressions by seeing where they originated in the first place and how the false understandings of how relationships worked were stuck in my belief system, I found myself with a massive passion and desire to share my newfound freedom and wholeness with the world.
>
> In the beginning I started speaking in mental health seminars and I noticed that almost everyone in the room could relate to what I was speaking about when I talked about this 'root belief system stuff' that had resulted from the messages that I got from the actions of adults in my childhood. I was seeing people's eyes pop open, and they were mobbing me on the breaks. It was really validating to have so many people interested in talking to me to learn more about how I found this new freedom from depression and how I recovered my self-esteem.
>
> I was in my mid-forties at this time and although I considered going back to school to become a therapist, I still had three kids at home and I lived way out in the country and could not figure out how I would attend school if I did go back, so I decided to become a professional coach. Since I was already working in the mental health arena, I chose a well-known American psychiatrist

who was the dean of a reputable coaching institute as my coaching instructor, so I could learn how to coach without crossing over into therapy.

Through coach training I learned about Internet marketing and began to read about how to get known through the Internet. The prospect of reaching a worldwide audience was exciting to me and armed with the confidence in my message that I was receiving as a mental health advocate and inspirational speaker, I started to take a few courses on how to get set up on the World Wide Web. I am not very techie. I barely knew how to cut and paste!

I was overwhelmed with all the possibilities, but I worked hard every day and downloaded every free training that I came across until I found the people that I really wanted to learn from and then I took a few actual Internet marketing courses. I determined from my studies that having a professional blog was the most effective way to present content and I took an online course with step-by-step instruction on starting a WordPress blog and I set up my website Emerging from Broken.com.

Although I had never considered myself a 'writer', I started writing about my journey to wholeness. I wrote small, consumable, bite-sized stories about how I discovered the false messages that were stuck in my brain because of the damage and trauma I had endured in my childhood. I wrote about sexual abuse, dissociative identity disorder, trauma, and depression. I wrote about my life and the solutions that I had found that helped me overcome the trauma in my own life. I learned about keywords, and Facebook and a few other social media mediums and learned how to get my content found and how to share it and how to get it shared and I started to get comments on my blog!

That was four and a half years ago now. My blog grew and grew and within two years I was averaging 1,000 legit comments a month and many of the comments were and still are over 2,000 words. I invited some experts to guest post, and I have invited people to share their own personal stories of healing. I have guest posted on other sites and commented on other blogs related to my blog topics, all of which helped me to increase my reach, which was my primary goal in the beginning!

I also built a successful private coaching practice through my blog. I have never advertised or posted that I had an opening (not even in Facebook) because I usually have a waiting list. I coach on the phone in Canada and the United States and on Skype in all other countries. Half (50%) of my clients are American and the other 50% are from all over the world.

Today the blog itself has over 400 posts and over 33,000 comments! When Emerging from Broken was about four months old I started a Facebook fan page and I have organically grown the following there to over 50,000 people, the Emerging from Broken Facebook page attracts an average of 100 new followers a day. I have become known as an expert on emotional healing and my website is read in 156 countries.

Most coaches and therapists have a passion to help people. That's why we do what we do and who doesn't want to reach a wider audience? I saw a problem in the world, and I believed I could contribute to the solution. I believed that I had unique information and I found a way to share it. I researched the best way to deliver this information and I learned how to do it. I celebrated the milestones along the way, and I persevered through the tough times. There was a time when I thought that building this whole thing took too long but when stop and think about it honestly, it's only been four and a half years and, in that time, have built a really high traffic website with hundreds of thousands of readers. I built a successful business; I have just published my first e-book 'Emerging from Broken ~ The Beginning of Hope for Emotional Healing' and I have a movie deal. I think that is pretty awesome! Hope and persistence mixed with passion plus courage and the willingness to share information has been the recipe that got me on the road to the where I am today.

There is beauty (and success) on the other side of broken.

(Ouimet, 2014)

Conclusion

Space prevents us from examining the myriad of other ways to provide CPD activities. For example, self-publishing is now easily done online and is more accepted as valid published resource. Self-published materials may range from coaching hand-outs as part of the work with the clients, to more hefty textbooks on your particular niche or style of coaching.

At the time of writing, it remains to be seen if the future of training and CPD will be recognisable in the traditional sense of it returning to being off-line. Whatever the case, it is extremely likely that the online environment will form a large proportion of such events, allowing us to spread expertise and information freely with our colleagues (within the legal parameters of copyright), and in turn learn from them about successful coaching practice techniques.

References

Anthony, K. (2014). 'Training Therapists to Work Effectively Online and Offline Within Digital Culture', *British Journal of Guidance and Counselling*. Published online.

hostingtribunal.com. (2021). *How Many Blogs Are There? We Counted Them All!!* https://hostingtribunal.com/blog/how-many-blogs/ [accessed 23 February 2021].

Johnstone, L. (2019). *What Is Continuing Professional Development (CPD)?* https://career-advice.jobs.ac.uk/career-development/what-is-continuing-professional-development-cpd/ [accessed 23 February 2021].

Ouimet, D. (2014). 'From Starting a Blog to Landing a Movie Deal ~ All on the WWW', *TILT Magazine*, Summer, pp. 14–18. https://issuu.com/onlinetherapyinstitute/docs/tilt-magazine_issue19_final2/5 [accessed 23 February 2021].

Wilson, J. and Anthony, K. (2015). 'Immersion Disinhibition: How the Internet Has Changed Our Learning', *TILT Magazine*, Winter, pp. 13–18.

Chapter 9

A look to the future and concluding thoughts

Introduction

Futurology is an inexact science at best, and a potentially dangerous one at worst. Much of the distrust and suspicion of using technology in the helping fields was, and often still is, positioned as 'computers taking over our jobs', or as something as fantastical as Star Trek. Douglas Adams puts this thus:

> *Trying to predict the future is a mug's game. But increasingly it's a game we all have to play because the world is changing so fast and we need to have some sort of idea of what the future's actually going to be like because we are going to have to live there, probably next week.*

> (Adams, 2002).

The reality is that technological development is unstoppable, and while some technologies may fall into disuse, or out of favour, some were robust enough in their original design to become permanent in our lives (such as email). Furthermore, to reject technology within our work may lead to a lack of empathetic skills when working with the client who embraces technology (much as the rest of the world).

As coaches, as well as therapists ourselves, we implore you to be among those who embrace technology. To complete your reading, we will look at some of the technologies that already exist for coaching work, and also speculate a little about what the future of coaching could look like.

Avatars

Avatars (representations of [in this context] human beings created by computer software) and Virtual Reality Environments have not been widely welcomed by the profession. In 2002, Goss and Anthony wrote:

> Whether 'avatar therapy' is to become one element of the future of counselling and psychotherapy is yet to be seen. But given the pace of developments

DOI: 10.4324/9781315685939-10

in the field it is impossible to rule it out and those practitioners with a tech-nological bent might do well to keep an eye open fields whatever uses it may, ultimately, be shown to have. What other innovations the technologists might have up their virtual sleeves we will have to wait and see.

This same field of possibilities applies to avatar coaching.

Avatar coaching is now a part of the 'future' discussed then, with coaching tak-ing place in the Massively Multiplayer Online (MMO) online platform Second Life (SL).

In SL at least, communication is made by typing on a keyboard (the avatar types onto air [an invisible keyboard] to indicate that the person is typing), and text appears above the avatar's head. Confidentiality is easily breached in this case as the text may be seen by anyone standing close enough to the conversation. This can be lessened by the use of a private, secure 'skybox', a private environment that is accessible only by those invited. Further enhancement of security may include the use of an encrypted chat/VoIP platform.

Chatrooms that use avatars or other visuals are similar to traditional chatrooms except that they allow the use of an avatar that can move around a virtual environ-ment. These can be used for anything from simple social networking with partici-pants talking to each other to playing a multiuser game such as World of Warcraft (WoW), where users band together to defeat enemies and achieve goals within the game. More sophisticated environments created by the user within a given platform offer even more, allowing whole communities to be built or the provi-sion of software to allow virtual sex. Some even offer their own commerce, such as Second Life where the currency – which can be converted to actual standard currencies offline – is Linden Dollars (L$).

According to Geissler and Kanatouri (2017), avatars can either be modelled or concrete with facial features, skin tones and clothing that may depict ethnicity and gender (such as those created in Second Life); or the avatar may be abstract fig-ures with no face or clothing such as with ProReal. The coach and the client may enter into the virtual world, or only the client enters. The virtual world environ-ment can be predetermined with a previously created landscape or may be created in real time. The coach and the client communicate via audio and chat.

Applications within ProReal include the following (Tinker, 2013) – clients can select a part of the landscape where they feel comfortable, or which represents their current situation. One client placed himself in the river with his family split on opposing banks. This act alone opened up a useful exploration of the reality of his home situation. Roads can be used as timelines and give the client an axis to move backwards and forwards in time. In a similar way to a therapist's use of 'Small World', a client can select avatars to represent people, entities, external stakeholders or sub-egos.

To enable the sociometry to become visible, the avatars can be positioned anywhere in the world and face any direction. In the programme in its simplest form, a client will position a number of avatars relative to each other, to represent a family or organisational situation, with the closest relationships next to one another and the most distant individuals further away, thus mapping out a system. The ways in which the world can be viewed are important as they enable perspectives on a paradigm. The design here was informed by Moreno's work (1889–1874) and, in particular, the value of seeing the world from another's perspective in order to build empathy. The platform enables the client to view the world from both the first person and the third person, thus broadening the options for perceiving. In addition, the world can be viewed from a free camera, meaning the client can step away from the system and view it from above (or indeed from any angle) in order to gain a different perspective. The purpose of this is to encourage new thinking, inspired by fresh ways of seeing things. One client has commented on the feeling of being able to 'fly' away from self and view the world from above.

The client's world can be shared either in person or remotely with a therapist or coach. The remote working function enables the coach to work with clients anywhere in the world. A client world in ProReal can be saved and returned to at a later session. It can also be accessed separately by the client, should personal reflection be valued.

One of the most exciting applications of avatar technology has been in the treatment of schizophrenia (Craig et al., 2018). According to the authors:

> AVATAR (sic) therapy (invented by Julian Leff in 2008) is a new approach in which people who hear voices have a dialogue with a digital representation (avatar) of their presumed persecutor, voiced by the therapist so that the avatar responds by becoming less hostile and concedes power over the course of therapy.
>
> (p. 1)

While the work of Leff et al. (2018) and colleagues is firmly rooted in psychiatric practice, we can be creative in our thinking as to how this may help our coachees. Tackling confidence issues and negative thoughts seems the most likely application within the coaching field, but we should not be limited by our imaginations or by a standard coaching practice that does not translate well to the online environment.

Hologram coaching

The use of hologram technology in the helping professions has not yet been tried or tested. What is interesting to consider is the application of a hologram technology that would return us to a face-to-face process. You may have seen hologram use on stage productions such as War of the Worlds (Wayne, 1978) or at music concerts, or at least heard reports of their use in the media.

Holograms are three-dimensional projections, and we recommend a search of YouTube for videos of examples. We have been considering the use of holograms in the helping professions for years now, but such technologies currently remain out of reach. Such projections do not have any tangible physical presence, so may be less useful for gaining the benefits of human touch that society has been used to pre-pandemic.

Conclusion

As well as the list of questions offered in the Introduction, these additional questions are posed as points for further consideration in Pascal *et al.* (2015):

1   Does the quality of the coaching experience suffer if technology is used to replace face-to-face coaching sessions entirely? In other words, rather than simply focusing on the addition of technology, is the absence of face-to-face interaction a detriment to the quality of coaching and important client outcomes?
2   We know that the relationship between coach and coachee is critical to the success of the coaching engagement. Can coach – coachees pairs cultivate an equally effective coaching relationship virtually as they can in person?
3   Do technology platforms (Skype, IM, etc.) present confidentiality or data security concerns? In other words, are there risks of others intentionally or unintentionally accessing coaching records, conversations, and so forth that are presumed to be private and confidential?

In 2021, many, if not the majority members of the helping professions still remember a time when the Internet had not been invented. This creates a unique time pinpoint in which to conduct important outcome comparison research for the online and off-line environments. We recommend the ongoing work of Therapy Meets Numbers for such comparisons (https://therapymeetsnumbers.com/), as much of the research in the therapeutic field is applicable to the coaching field.

To conclude, we invite you to reconsider the questions in our introduction to this book, which we hope are helpful in examining where you sit on the technology-in-coaching spectrum. Pascal's questions in the above paragraph are more anthropological in nature and would fit well within a peer group discussion, whether conducted in an online or an off-line space. These introductory questions will also be useful for the purposes of self-evaluation of your competency to work online – skills that are likely to be instrumental in your future career. We wish you the best in your endeavours for a successful and effective coaching practice.

References

Adams, D. (2002). *The Salmon of Doubt*. New York: Del Ray.
Craig, T., *et al.* (2018). 'Avatar Therapy for Auditory Verbal Hallucinations in People with Psychosis: A Single Blind Randomised Controlled Trial', *The Lancet*, 5(1), pp. 31–40. www.thelancet.com/journals/lanpsy/article/PIIS2215-0366(17)30427-3/fulltext?elsca1=tlpr [accessed 25 February 2021].

Geissler, H. and Kanatouri, S. (2017). 'Coaching Through Modern Media', in A. Schreyögg and C. Schmidt-Lellek (eds.), *The Professionalization of Coaching*. Wiesbaden: Springer. https://doi.org/10.1007/978-3-658-16805-6_19 [accessed 25 February 2021].

Leff, J., *et al.* (2018). *Computer-assisted Therapy for Medication-resistant Auditory Hallucinations: Proof-of-concept Study*. Published online by Cambridge University Press. www.cambridge.org/core/journals/the-british-journal-of-psychiatry/article/computerassisted-therapy-for-medicationresistant-auditory-hallucinations-proofofconcept-study/AB7E2C95BCB72A3CA1092F2F2E39FC6A [accessed 25 February 2021].

Pascal, A., Sass, M. and Gregory, J.B. (2015). 'I'm Only Human: The Role of Technology in Coaching', *Consulting Psychology Journal: Practice and Research*, 67(2), p. 100.

Tinker, D. (2013). 'Unlocking the Client's Internal Dialogue with Virtual Reality', *Therapeutic Innovations in Light of Technology*, 3(3), pp. 22–29.

Wayne, J. (1978). *Jeff Wayne's Musical Version of the War of the Worlds; a Concept Album*. Columbia/CBS Records, Advision Studios, London, UK.

Index

Printed in the United States
by Baker & Taylor Publisher Services